Defoe:
Writer as Agent

KATHERINE A. ARMSTRONG

Defoe:
Writer as Agent

English Literary Studies
University of Victoria
1996

ENGLISH LITERARY STUDIES
Published at the University of Victoria

Founding Editor
Samuel L. Macey

GENERAL EDITOR
Robert M. Schuler

EDITORIAL BOARD
Thomas R. Cleary
Evelyn M. Cobley
Kathryn Kerby-Fulton
Victor A. Neufeldt
Stephen A. C. Scobie

ADVISORY EDITORS
David Fowler, *University of Washington*
Donald Greene, *University of Southern California*
Juliet McMaster, *University of Alberta*
Richard J. Schoeck, *University of Colorado*
Arthur Sherbo, *Michigan State University*

BUSINESS MANAGER
Hedy Miller

ISBN 0-920604-86-2

The ELS Monograph Series is published in consultation with members of the Department by ENGLISH LITERARY STUDIES, Department of English, University of Victoria, P.O. Box 3070, Victoria, B.C., Canada, v8w 3w1.

ELS Monograph Series No. 67
© 1996 by Katherine A. Armstrong

The cover shows a portrait of Daniel Defoe from the chapbook, pirated edition of *Jure Divino* (1706), reproduced in Paula R. Backscheider, *Daniel Defoe: His Life* © 1989. Reprinted by permission of the Johns Hopkins University Press.

CONTENTS

ACKNOWLEDGMENTS

Part of Chapter Three originally appeared, in modified form, in *Tradition in Transition: Women Writers, Marginal Texts, and the Eighteenth-Century Canon*, eds. Alvaro Ribeiro and James G. Basker (Oxford: Clarendon, 1995).

I am grateful to the John Rylands Research Institute for a grant that greatly facilitated the research of this book, and to Chester College for a period of research leave which enabled me to complete the writing of it. I am also grateful to the libraries of the University of California, Berkeley, Stanford University Library, the library of the University of Bristol, the John Rylands Library, the University of Manchester, Manchester City Library and Chester College Library.

Special thanks are due to Ian Watt, who offered invaluable insights at the earliest stages of the project, and to Alvaro Ribeiro and James G. Basker for editing a previous version of Chapter Three. I should also like to thank Paula Backscheider for her advice concerning the authorship of *A New Voyage Round the World*.

Like all students of Defoe, I owe much to earlier historians and literary scholars. Although the bibliography at the end of this study lists only those directly cited, I should like to register here my general debt to those whose works I have consulted in the course of my research.

Two undergraduate research assistants spent a summer tracking down references and compiling bibliographies, and I am grateful to them: Richard Juang of Stanford University and Kerry Marsh of Chester College.

My greatest debts are to the editor and copy-editor of English Literary Studies, who have been unstintingly generous with their time and scholarship in helping to prepare this book for publication.

Lastly, my thanks to Andrew Mortlock, whose idea it was to go to San Francisco in the first place.

A NOTE ON TEXTS

In choosing editions of major texts from which I quote extensively, I have aimed for the reader's convenience rather than for consistency. For *Memoirs of a Cavalier*, *Captain Singleton* and *Colonel Jack*, therefore, I have used the Oxford World's Classics editions, while I have cited the Penguin editions of *Moll Flanders* and *Robinson Crusoe*.

INTRODUCTION

On 18 March 1707 Daniel Defoe was in Scotland, working as a spy on behalf of Robert Harley and doing all in his powers to promote the Union. For once his letter to his employer is excited and confident, presumably because the latest skirmish in the pamphlet war has just produced a victory for which "the Moderate Men of the Clergy Come Every Day to thank [him]." Defoe's enthusiasm for his role is manifest:

> In my Mannagemt here I am a perfect Emissary. I act the Old part of Cardinall Richlieu. I have my spyes and my Pensioners In Every place, and I Confess 'tis the Easyest thing in the World to hire people here to betray their friends. I have spies in the Commission, in the parliament, and in the assembly, and Undr pretence of writeing my hystory I have Every Thing told me.[1]

The passage is frequently quoted by biographers and critics, partly because it confirms the traditional view of the "protean" Defoe which is associated with J. R. Moore in particular,[2] a view which has come under attack from the revisionist bibliographic work of P. N. Furbank and W. R. Owens,[3] yet remains a virtual commonplace of Defoe criticism. Michael McKeon, for example, alludes to "the remarkable vicissitudes and duplicities of Daniel Defoe's . . . career,"[4] and Paula Backscheider points out that Defoe himself is responsible for the judgment that his work has been "all things to all men."[5] In fact it would seem that Defoe's versatility has been one of his chief attractions for twentieth-century commentators. Peter Earle, for example, begins *The World of Defoe* by describing the challenges posed by tackling this most chameleon-like of writers:

> Certainly, if some of Defoe's works were not illustrations of his own life, the biography is going to be rather thin. But what does one select? And from which books? From the novels or from the didactic works? Was Defoe like Robinson Crusoe or the Complete English Tradesman, like Moll Flanders or like the repentant father in the first volume of *The Family Instructor*? Was he an adventurer or was he a rational economic man, was he obsessed with sex or with salvation; was he all of them or none of them? The scope is wide.[6]

9

Yet in focusing so intently on the dissimulations evident in Defoe's life and works we have tended to overlook a further significance in his perception of himself as a "Cardinall Richlieu." To work as an agent is, as the etymology of the word suggests, to *act* in both senses of the word; firstly, to adopt a role, and second, to participate in the public sphere, albeit secretively. Defoe's urgent desire to take part in the political and economic life of his country is the subject of this book, which hopes to show that by setting to one side our longstanding preoccupation with the veracity or, conversely, the fictiveness of Defoe's prose narratives (and, by extension, of Defoe himself), and by examining them instead as conscious interventions in various contemporary political debates, we transform our readings of them.

The texts on which I have chosen to concentrate all date from the "mature" phase of Defoe's literary career, the period between 1719 and 1722. These years saw the publication of his works best-known to twentieth-century readers, *Robinson Crusoe* (1719) and *Moll Flanders* (1722). Recent critical discussions of Defoe have tended to focus primarily on his technical mastery of the fictive possibilities of an emergent genre, the novel, and they have therefore devoted special attention to these texts, which are the most obviously novelistic in his oeuvre. Thus of *Robinson Crusoe*'s achievements in representing human psychology McKeon comments that "Defoe gives to the notion of the true history of the individual so intimate and introspective a form that it comes close to looking more like self-creation" (337). As Lennard Davis says, "Countless anthologies and critical works begin here at the famous landmark of the literary pilgrimage, and one always hears first the strange story of the industrious man on the island who spends his days listing his provisions and walling himself deeper into his isolation against a danger that fails to materialize for twenty years."[7]

In a sense, however, such views are dangerously teleological in assuming that Defoe got better and better at using the novel genre and that his most successful works are those which come closest to "imaginative literature." The contemporaneity of the other texts I shall discuss—*Memoirs of a Cavalier* (1720), *Captain Singleton* (1720), and *Colonel Jack* (1722)—with the previous two I listed undermines the case for a Whiggish view of Defoe's development as a novelist. Moreover, representing a range of genres, from novels to pseudo-autobiographies to travel writing, they illustrate that any distinction between Defoe's "major" and "minor" novels on the grounds of fictiveness is an artificial and misleading one. In all of them the categories of fact and fiction are blurred provocatively and artfully, alerting us to the fact that Defoe's nar-ratological experiments were driven by pragmatic rather than aesthetic considerations. The thesis I wish to propose here is that Defoe blended fact and fiction throughout his career as an author (but arguably most effectively and subtly in the late 1710s and early to mid-1720s) for covert and overt political ends. His celebrated circumstantiality, for example, can be seen to stem not from a conscious desire for novelistic innovation but from the necessity to convert and convince; typically he tended to follow up a bold generalisation with an overwhelming pleth-ora of detail. Like a new reading of *Robinson Crusoe* which relates it to the Glorious Revolution,[8] a historicist interpretation of *Roxana* which has highlighted its obliquely satirical references to the Hanoverian court,[9] and a recent study of Defoe's remodelling of the criminal biography,[10] this study will suggest that literary critics have, with some exceptions, been too eager to emphasize Defoe's role as father of the modern English novel, and too inclined to overlook the political motives for his artistic practice.

It may well be, of course, that critics have paid relatively less attention to Defoe's overtly politicized narratives for precisely this reason: the Romantic impulse to portray him in retrospect as a writer who gradually rose above the ephemeral world of politics and became absorbed in the extraordinary possibilities offered by the novel. Such an impulse is likely to diminish, given current critical preoccupations with the political significance of literature generally. Yet most recent accounts of the "rise of the novel" continue to explore the interrelations of fact and fiction in the "new" genre and to try to comprehend what was new about prose narratives in the early eighteenth century, in primarily narratological and epistemological terms.[11] In offering correctives to traditional read-ings of literary history one must resist crudely caricaturing the positions of other critics. It should be remembered, for example, that Ian Watt was in no sense suggesting that Defoe's contribution to the rise of individualism was born out of a proto-Romantic introspection; the individualism of Defoe's protagonists was, for Watt, intimately bound up with the economic changes taking place in early modern England.[12] For Davis political pressures were behind the divergent directions taken by "factual" news and the novel in the early eighteenth century, and Defoe exemplifies the split. Nonetheless, critics have undoubtedly tended to privilege Defoe's "major novels" over the rest of his works and to see these as transcending their times in a way which certain of his other writings do not. In reply I would suggest that none of Defoe's texts should be divorced from its context; that all of them are highly resourceful in drawing on the rhetorical strategies associated with fiction and non-fiction respectively; and that they do so precisely because they are rooted in specific political controversies rather than because they seek to create an autonomous realm of the imagination.

This book, then, offers an exposition of Defoe's methods in five of his most important works, and its overriding aim will be to account for those methods rather than simply to describe them. By way of exemplification I will conclude my introduction with an examination of one short text which bears out these claims for contextualisation and which, moreover, illustrates that fictiveness is by no means exclusive to Defoe's later works. First, however, Defoe's political background ought to be delineated, though the sweeping judgments I offer here will pass muster only in the light of the detailed analysis of subsequent chapters. Nonetheless, I should say at this early point that I am sceptical of the notion that Defoe's political views were so much determined by expediency that we cannot define them with any certainty. It has been in the interests of those commited to expanding the Defoe canon to consider him capable of the most barefaced reversals and deceptions, but in fact his political sympathies were broadly consistent throughout his career and are by no means ambiguous except in the sense that he found a bewildering variety of ways to convey them. They are much less difficult to summarize than one might assume, though the complexities of post-Restoration politics and the indeterminate nature of political parties in the period mean that it is more fruitful to discuss Defoe's adherence to certain causes and his hostility to others than to search for a single term such as "Williamite" or "Dissenting" or even a compound label such as "Whig-Protestant" to describe him.

Briefly, then, Defoe supported the Protestant Succession and, in particular, William III; he was, therefore, keen to promote the 1701 Act of Settlement and, later, to defend the Hanoverians. These allegiances remained firm throughout his career, being evident in his many pamphlets on the Succession and in passing allusions embedded in almost all his other works. In religion he was a nonconformist; though there is no evidence to link him with the Quaker movement, he was educated at a Dissenting academy and attended various meeting-houses for Dissenters from his childhood onwards. It was largely this background which accounts for another dominant theme in his writing, the benefits of the union between England and Scotland. Defoe thought that the Scottish church had much in common with the English nonconformists and that an Act of Union would quash all Stuart pretensions to the Scottish throne.

He was, therefore, well disposed towards the Scots, particularly the Cameronians of the Lowlands, though he was implacably opposed to the Highland Jacobites and often articulated contemporary popular prejudices about the corruption of Scottish officials (these were very likely born out of resentment at the clandestine trade carried on in the Scottish ports before the Union legalized exports and imports with the colonies).[13] But another factor in his Unionism was his staunch commitment to the commercial interests of the two kingdoms, both of which he believed would profit from the resulting new trade agreements.

His identification with the commercial interest as opposed to that of the court very likely reflects his mercantile background and early career, and is reflected in his many essays in defence of William's Continental campaigns. Most merchants supported William's aggressive stance towards Louis XIV, largely because French onslaughts on the English navy were deleterious to England's trade. Commercialism underlies Defoe's conviction that England should defend the "Balance of Europe," resistance to Bourbon expansionism being especially crucial in maintaining stable relations between the European states. His commercial outlook also accounts for his lifelong belief in the colonies as a source of almost limitless wealth for the mother country.

There were corresponding dislikes. Defoe's antipathy towards Roman Catholicism is discernible in almost everything he wrote. It explains his attacks on religious and monarchical absolutism, and his highly critical view of the Stuarts and their Jacobite supporters, and partly explains his resentment of Spain and Italy, as well as France. Spain and France were, of course, England's rivals in the New World, so that Defoe's anti-Catholicism was at least partly economic in origin. In several of his works he compares England's dilatory approach to colonisation with the go-getting style of the Spanish.

Other ideological biases are, of course, identifiable. For example, rather like modern-day Democratic presidential candidates, Defoe was fiscally conservative and socially liberal. He argued for a number of enlightened policies, including education for women and state care for the elderly,[14] but he was an old-fashioned mercantilist who wanted the government to hold on to its bullion reserves and promote export overseas. Neither was he exactly progressive when it came to crime, though his solution—mass transportation overseas—was in some regards more humanitarian than official policies of the time. His opinions on trade and commerce are now considered to have been somewhat outdated, but he had a reasonable grasp of the principal problems facing England and Scotland, and attempted at various times to formulate rational solutions to them.

If this summary is accurate, Defoe's reputation as a "Proteus" would seem largely undeserved, though it can be attributed to two factors. Firstly, the checklist of writings assigned to Defoe by J. R. Moore is so lengthy and diverse that those who have accepted it have not surprisingly tended to conclude that Defoe must have cynically written for any party who would hire him. This suspicion is confirmed by the fact that he continued to support Robert Harley after Harley's defection from the Whigs to the Tories. Second, Defoe's ability to portray fictional characters convincingly "from within" has prompted suspicions about his overall sincerity. The creation of authentic fictional characters was indeed much rarer in the early eighteenth century than it would later become; nonetheless it seems unfair to question Defoe's own honesty on the grounds that he created remarkably true-to-life protagonists. Feminist critics have recently taken issue with the conventional view that Aphra Behn was trying to deceive the readers of *Oroonoko* (1688) when she told them she had been to Surinam herself. Isn't the novel as a genre all about the reader's suspension of disbelief, such critics have asked.[15] A similar question might be put to Defoe's critics, though perhaps because he was not trying to usurp a realm of masculine privilege Defoe has been more often praised than condemned for the verisimilitude of his characters and settings.

In any case, a reader unfamiliar with the notion of an infinitely "versatile" Defoe is, I think, more likely to be struck by the consistency with which his sympathies and animosities were maintained over a writing career spanning more than thirty years than to be troubled by his supposed trimming. David Macaree has shown that anti-Jacobitism is a guiding principle for Defoe throughout his life,[16] and since anti-Jacobitism is ultimately connected with virtually all his other allegiances—to Protestantism, to Holland as an ally against France and Spain, to the merchant interest as the source of national wealth, and so on—there are no rational grounds for continuing to foster the image of Defoe as a counterfeiting upstart who repeatedly changed sides with an eye to the main chance. As I hope to show in what follows, Defoe's political beliefs were coherent in themselves, though their expression was sometimes deliberately equivocal.

To support my argument that political aims are central to Defoe's development of various narratological strategies—in other words, that they are the reason for his characteristic manipulations of fact and fiction—I shall conclude this introduction with an analysis of the work for which he was perhaps best-known to his contemporaries, the polemical poem *The True-Born Englishman* (1701).[17] A number of reasons govern this choice. Firstly, *The True-Born Englishman* articulates clearly all the important beliefs which characterize Defoe's work, so it serves as a helpful introduction to tracing his political profile. It also testifies to the necessity of reading Defoe's works in their social and political context: even more than his prose works it clamours for annotation, thereby demonstrating the advantages of the approach adopted in the rest of this study. Lastly, it indicates both the extent to which Defoe was prepared to blend fact and fiction and why he did so. When we read *The True-Born Englishman* we are bound to ask how we may define generically a text which is a pamphlet but also a poem, a fierce satire as well as a recitation of historical facts, and an invective which is delivered in the service of reason and tolerance. Compared with the infinitely subtle ironies of the later prose works, *The True-Born Englishman* is a straightforward affair, but this is exactly its usefulness: it vividly illustrates the need to consider the intentions underlying Defoe's rhetoric as well as the rhetoric itself. Irony and technical virtuosity are not employed merely for their own sakes.

The True-Born Englishman was published in response to a pamphlet attack on William III as a "Foreigner" by the maverick Whig, John Tutchin (1661?-1707).[18] As Backscheider, Defoe's most recent biographer, puts it, *The True-Born Englishman* was to become his "signature" (*Defoe: His Life* 75), running to numerous editions and prompting at least three replies.[19] It is in two main parts, with a Preface and an Explanatory Preface which was added to later editions, and has approximately 1200 lines.

Located in the often obscure pamphlet wars of the early eighteenth century, and making veiled and not so veiled references to a number of now forgotten historical figures, *The True-Born Englishman* is today sometimes difficult to evaluate. Its significance and its complexity are, however, inextricably linked, for it demonstrates Defoe's skill as a polemicist at a relatively early stage in his writing career and thus anticipates the inventiveness of many of his later prose narratives, with their readiness to blend fact and fiction, symbolism and circumstantiality. For here Defoe deploys irony, allegory, myth, axiom, biblical allusion and nationalist trope alongside references to real people and events of recent history, all in the service of his pro-Revolution agenda. The poem is famous as an early retort to specious nationalism, but it is even more remarkable for its curious blend of tolerance and xenophobia. Defoe offers an assault on English insularity, but he does not entirely deliver it. On the one hand he seems to scorn the coarse patriotism of his time; on the other, he seems to play on it. I would, therefore, question Christopher Hill's claim that it belongs to a literary tradition of "freedom"; more relevant would seem to be Hill's generalisation that "Our literature contains an eerie combination of [nationalist] humbug with savage irony at humbug's expense."[20]

The following reading of the poem attempts to explain its profound and disappointing contradictions by placing it in the context of contemporary political controversies. In deciphering the political and sectarian messages encoded in each of Defoe's "mature" prose works, it will be profitable to begin with the question, What, if anything, was this text trying to achieve, ideologically speaking? With *The True-Born Englishman* I have the same question in mind, the answer to which accounts for the inconsistency of Defoe's argument—his "eerie combination of humbug with savage irony at humbug's expense"—and the variety of techniques he uses to advance it.

The poem begins in a promisingly oppositional vein, Defoe's Explanatory Preface (which, though written later, appears first) combatively denying that its purpose is to retract anything in his text, and his Preface (printed second) recalling Swift's opening to *The Battle of the Books* (1697): "The End of Satyr is Reformation" (A3v).[21] The characteristically tendentious tone is substantiated by a stout refusal to countenance popular prejudices about, respectively, the innate superiority of the English (*"Why should not our Neighbours be as good as we to Derive from?"* [A2]); the desirability of racial "purity" (*"those Nations which are most mixed are the best"* [A2]); the value of ancestral pedigrees ("What they would infer from their long Original, I know not" [A2]); and the lowness of foreigners ("speaking of *Englishmen ab origine,* we are really all Foreigners our selves" [A2v]). In the poem itself Defoe proceeds from a narration of England's heterogeneous past to an anatomy of the English character (rash, drunken and ungracious, among other things) to a set speech in which Britannia personifies that segment of the population sensible of its debt to William and willing to express it. In the savagely satirical conclusion an unnamed (but easily identifiable) public representative of the true-born Englishman cheerfully describes his meteoric career, and the electoral and financial corruption it has involved.

The central irony of the poem is the hostility of the English to foreigners, their Dutch-born king in particular, given that their country's long history of invasion, conquest and assimilation has produced "a Race uncertain and unev'n, / Deriv'd from all the Nations under Heav'n" (6). Defoe's dismissive response to the notion of a stable and unchanging English identity is almost startling, anticipating the cosmopolitanism we instinctively, if erroneously, associate with our own century. Defoe is sarcastic about the discontent arising from William's rewards to his favourites, Portland and Schomberg, pointing out that these reviled foreigners have promoted English national interests tirelessly and that criticisms of them are motivated purely by jealousy: "'Tis not at Foreigners that we repine, / Would Foreigners their Perquisites resign" (1). As well as cataloguing the myriad faults he sees in the English, which, tongue-in-cheek, he attributes to their history of miscegenation—"All these their Barb'rous Off-spring left behind, / The Dregs of Armies, they of all Mankind / Blended with *Britains* who before were here, / Of whom the *Welsh* ha' blest the Character" (6)—Defoe also rejects the myth of a pure English language. Such a myth is a powerful tool of nationalism, as Elie Kedourie, among others, argues,[22] but it is also one which is contradicted by empirical observation:

> The Customs, Sir-names, Languages, and Manners,
> Of all these Nations are their own Explainers;
> Whose Relicks are so lasting and so strong,
> They've left a *Shiboleth* upon our Tongue;
> By which, with easie search, you may distinguish
> Your Roman-Saxon-Danish-Norman English.   (6)

In concluding Part One of the poem Defoe points out that for all the English's pride in tracing lines of descent back to ancient times, most of the English peerage are of foreign origin ("S[ackvi]lls, S[avi]s, C[eci]ls, D[ela]M[e]rs, / M[ohun]s, M[ontag]ues, D[ura]s, and V[ee]r[e]s, / Not one have *English* names"), while the Continental extraction of many prominent commoners is equally evident: "Your H[oublo]ns, P[apil]lons, and L[ethieul]iers / Pass now for *True-Born-English* knights and squires" (12).[23] This attack on the country's ruling classes is part of Defoe's larger project to expose those who question the legitimacy of William to rule the English. Towards the end of the poem corruption in the city of London will be subjected to examination; here, at the end of Part One, the established church is accused of hypocrisy in having affirmed the doctrine of non-resistance only to have solicited William's help once James began to threaten the security of the church's assets; worse still,

17

the Anglican clergy has now turned against William, too, the danger of popery having passed.

Defoe recognises the potency of certain national myths, language included, and their inability to withstand scrutiny. Thus the liberty of which the English are famously so proud is actually licence to drunkenness (14); the courage provided by their famous English beef is mere rashness, erratically maintained; and the legendary "plain English" is all too often "English Billingsgate" (A3). He continues in this anti-xenophobic vein: Part Two of the poem identifies so many weaknesses in the English people that it can be read as a provocative attempt to define Englishness as a compound of all the national vices listed in Part One: Spanish pride (like the haughty Spaniards the English "hate to see themselves oblig'd too much" [16]); Italian lustfulness (though English women in Defoe's eyes are tempted by "want of Money more than Inclination" [18][24]); German drunkenness; French inconstancy ("And if they're not Vindictive in their Fury, / 'Tis their Un-constant Temper does secure-ye" [17]).

Yet within this self-conscious appropriation of the fallacies and clichés beloved of nationalism, we begin to see the limitations of Defoe's own tolerance. Scornful of the dogma of ethnic purity on the one hand, he is happy to rehearse essentialist arguments when they suit his purposes. Not only does each nation have its "proper Sins" (3) (here, of course, "proper" is being used in the obsolete sense of "own"), but such sins are overtly linked to popular stereotypes. The devil enslaves every nation differently:

> By Zeal the *Irish*, and the *Rush* by folly,
> Fury the *Dane*, the *Swede* by Melancholly;
> By stupid Ignorance, the *Muscovite*;
> The *Chinese* by a Child of Hell, call'd Wit;
> Wealth makes the *Persian* too Effeminate;
> And Poverty the *Tartars* Desperate;
> The *Turks* and *Moors*, by *Mah'met* he subdues;
> *And God has giv'n him leave to rule the* Jews;
> Rage rules the *Portuguese*, and Fraud the *Scotch*;
> Revenge the *Pole*; and Avarice the *Dutch*.   (5)

Such enthusiasm for the caricatures of contemporary racist discourse surely undermines the claim that *The True-Born Englishman* is an un-problematic critique of xenophobia. The poem's title is a clue to its paradoxical aims: to reveal the absurdity of current assertions of national identity, whilst at the same time proposing a normative Englishness of Defoe's own defining. The end of *The True-Born Englishman* discards traditional conceptions of the English character in favour of one which is meritocratic and anti-traditionalist but no less heroic and sentimental than its predecessor:

> Cou'd but our Ancestors retrieve their Fate,
> And see their Off-spring thus Degenerate;
> How we contend for Birth and Names Unknown,
> And Build on their past Actions, not our own;
> They'd Cancel Records, and Their Tombs Deface,
> And openly disown the Vile Degenerate Race;
> For Fame of Families is all a Cheat,
> *'Tis Personal Vertue only makes us Great.*   (32)

The same idealism underpins the poem's portrait of Sir Charles Duncombe, whose identity must have been transparent, though he is not actually named, and whose career Defoe uses to illustrate the corruption at the heart of English society, the city of London in particular. Defoe gives Duncombe a speech which counterpoints the generous outpouring of praise and thanks to William by "Britannia" in the preceding section. "Britannia" is an allegorical figure borrowed from the literature of eighteenth-century "radical patriotism,"[25] and the appearance of Sir Charles Duncombe is equally rhetorical or "fictive," reflecting Defoe's political bias more than it does any desire for historical accuracy. "Britannia" symbolizes the ideal, Duncombe the shocking reality.

Duncombe (d. 1711) is described by the *Dictionary of National Biography* as a banker and politician, and, as Defoe points out, he was of lowly origins (though not, perhaps, from labouring stock, as *The True-Born Englishman* would have it). He rose to become one of the richest men in England and did indeed, as Defoe claims, stand for mayoral office in 1700, winning the highest number of votes. He was, however, subsequently rejected in favour of Sir Thomas Abney (1640-1722) (another of Defoe's enemies),[26] presumably because of the notorious financial scandal which had culminated in Duncombe's trial for forgery in 1699: he was found not guilty, it would seem, only on a technicality.

As Defoe sardonically notes, Duncombe made a famous donation to the church of St. Magnus ("Great Monuments of Charity he raises, / *And good* St. Magnus *whistles out his Praises*" [28]) and released many prisoners from London's debtors' prisons during his term as sheriff (unlike Gulielmus Hogaeus, Defoe saw nothing admirable in this popular gesture).[27] But clearly he was intimately involved in the corrupt public life which Defoe regarded as a major threat to his country's peace and prosperity. Not only had Duncombe stood trial; he had also abandoned his master, Edward Backwell (d.1683), when Backwell got into financial difficulties (a betrayal Defoe somewhat hyperbolically likens to those of Judas Iscariot and the traitor Ziba, who misrepresented Mephibosheth, son of Jonathan, to David [2 Sam. 9:2]). He was a likely figure to have antagonised Defoe, since he had lent support to, and presumably profited hugely from, the administrations of Charles II and James II. In 1688, however, foreseeing James's end, he refused to lend him £1,500 in exile, and by 1689 he had advanced a loan of £20,000 to William and Mary.[28] Defoe's fictionalized Duncombe gloats at his ability to manage kings and sequester public funds:

> In our late Revolution 'twas thought strange
> That I of all Mankind shou'd like the Change,
> But they who wonder'd at it, never knew,
> That in it I did my old Game pursue:
> Nor had they heard of Twenty thousand Pound,
> Which never was lost, nor ne'er was found.   (31)

Duncombe was utterly unscrupulous and yet was securely lodged in the highest circles of the land. He had not only made a shrewd donation to the established church, but he was supported at his trial by three of the most powerful men in the government, Nottingham, Rochester and Leeds[29] (Leeds himself was associated with financial skulduggery in office).[30] Defoe would not have been surprised that Duncombe would, eventually, be elected lord mayor (in 1708). For Defoe he provides an insight into national abuses which points up William's probity all the more sharply, so that although his portrayal of him is indeed consonant with the historical facts, it is by no means disinterested or free of nationalist sentiments.

Defoe's stance is that of the relentlessly probing satirist who can expose as "empty" the phrase "true-born Englishman" when applied to the likes of Duncombe, yet his intention is to dissociate English nationalism from the less salubrious aspects of English society rather than to destroy the intellectual credibility of nationalism itself. He uses Duncombe to expose a crucial inconsistency in the position of William's critics. Indifferent when it came to "true-born" individuals such as Duncombe, many contemporaries were vociferous in their attacks on William's "foreign" favourites, Portland and Schomberg. Herein lies Defoe's own illogicality, for he is not offering to dispense with national heroes altogether but to substitute his own in place of those who had been favoured by the Stuart courts. As he bitterly notes, attacks on Portland and Schomberg are wholly self-seeking: "The Grand Contention's plainly to be seen, / To get some Men put out, and some put in" (1). Foreign supporters of the state, he points out, have been among *"the greatest Additions to the Wealth and Strength of the Nation"* (A2v), and William's favourites are wholly entitled to their perquisites. William Bentinck, 1st Earl of Portland (1649-1709), was indeed entrusted with the secrets of the king's foreign policy, and given large estates in the wake of the Revolution, but as Defoe says, he was invaluable in uncovering the secret intentions of James II, and fought for William at the Battle of the Boyne.[31] Frederick Hermann, 1st Duke of Schomberg (1615-1690), actually gave his life at the Boyne and had impeccable Protestant credentials, having fought against the Imperialists in the Thirty Years War, suffered exile after the revocation of the Edict of Nantes in 1685, and served under the Elector of Brandenburg as well as William before being made commander-in-chief in Ireland.[32]

In commemorating Schomberg Defoe is at his most exclamatory and jingoistic:

> Schombergh, the Ablest Soldier of his Age,
> With great *Nassau* did in our Cause engage;
> Both joyn'd for *England*'s Rescue and Defence,
> *The Greatest Captain and the Greatest Prince.* (27)

We are supposed to contrast this heroic figure with the sordid Duncombe, ambitious purely for his own sake. Interestingly, although Defoe is at pains to emphasize rather than deny Schomberg's foreignness (and that of William's other advisers, "Strangers, *Germans, Huguonots,* and *Dutch*" [28]), he presents him as the epitome of English chivalry in his patriotism (he fought not for William but for "*England*'s Rescue and Defence"), courage and loyalty. This is not to concede anything so silly as that chivalry is the prerogative of the English, merely that Defoe is more than willing to exploit a mythology of aristocratic valour which would have had an emotive appeal for his readers.[33]

It is a mythology Defoe also invokes later in the poem, despite his trenchant observation on the present nobility, that "from some *French* Trooper they derive, / Who with the *Norman* Bastard did arrive" (7). The implication, however incoherently expressed, is always that the present sorry lot represent a decline in national standards. In words which are very like those which would appear in a similarly satirical attack on Charles II,[34] Defoe accuses the Stuarts rather than William of giving the real encouragement to foreign usurpers:

21

The Royal Refugee our Breed restores,
With Foreign Courtiers, and with Foreign Whores;
And carefully repeopled us again,
Throughout his Lazy, Long, Lascivious Reign,
With such a blest and True-born English Fry,
As much Illustrates our Nobility.
A Gratitude which will so black appear,
As future Ages must abhor to bear:
When they look back on all that Crimson Flood,
Which streamed in Lindsey's, and Caernarvon's Blood;
Bold Strafford [sic], Cambridge, Capel, Lucas, Lisle,
Who crown'd in Death his Father's Fun'ral Pile.
The Loss of whom, in order to supply
With True-Born English N[obili]ty,
Six Bastard Dukes survive his Luscious Reign,
The Labours of Italian C[astlemai]n[e],
French P[ortsmout]h, Tabby S[co]t and Cambrian;
Besides the Num'rous Bright and Virgin Throng,
Whose Female Glories shade them from my Song.
This Off-spring, if one Age they multiply,
May half the House with English Peers supply:
There with true English Pride they may contemn
S[chomber]g and P[ortlan]d, new-made Noblemen.   (9)

The charge that Charles was too susceptible to the influences of the French and their mores after his exile in Paris was commonly made in the period,[35] and incidentally survives in, for example, literary histories which lay undue stress on the French influence on Restoration drama.[36] There was something in the idea; after all, Charles did have mistresses who were French, though more who were English. But for Defoe the issue is in no doubt, and the image of a smoking pile of dead English lords, the victims of Stuart tyranny, is presented in shocking contrast to the present nobility, swollen by the six sons and several daughters on whom Charles conferred titles.[37]

Defoe's targets may be identified as follows: "Italian Castlemaine" is Barbara Palmer, countess of Castlemaine, later duchess of Cleveland, by whom Charles had three sons—Charles Fitzroy, created duke of Southampton and Portsmouth; Henry Fitzroy, created duke of Grafton; and George Fitzroy, created duke of Northumberland. "French Portsmouth" is Louise de Querouaille, duchess of Portsmouth, whose son by Charles, Charles Lennox, was made duke of Richmond. "Tabby Scot" is presumably Lucy Walters, the mother of James Scott, duke of Monmouth.

"Tabby" is recorded as a pejorative term for unmarried women later in the eighteenth century,[38] and Lucy was the target of much amusement since Charles never gave her the legal marriage she wanted. "Cambrian" must, therefore, refer to Nell Gwyn, who was reputed to have been born in the Welsh border town of Hereford and who bore Charles two sons, the eldest of whom, Charles Beauclerk, became duke of St. Albans. Though all this was common knowledge, Defoe's fidelity to detail is impressive; for instance, another son, Charles Fitzcharles (by Catharine Peg), was made earl of Plymouth rather than having a dukedom conferred on him and is, therefore, omitted from Defoe's tally.[39]

Clearly the loyalists who chafe under a "foreign" king have little to be proud of in a reign in which "*French* Cooks, *Scotch* Pedlars, and *Italian* Whores, / Were all made L[or]ds or L[or]ds Progenitors" (9). Defoe's argument is persuasive even if couched in somewhat repellent terms. The crudity and aggression of this passage should, however, prompt us to look more critically at the instances of racist invective in *The True-Born Englishman* and consider their significance for a poem which has traditionally been admired for tolerance.

Like almost all Defoe's works, *The True-Born Englishman* is hostile towards the French and Italians. Castlemaine and Portsmouth are singled out, partly because they were among the most prominent of Charles's mistresses, but also because they represented the Catholic empires of France and Rome and underscored Charles II's sympathies for them. (Lucy Walters and Nell Gwyn, by virtue of their Scots and Welsh associations, neatly undermine Tory loyalist appeals to a monolithic English national identity.) For Defoe it is intolerable that William III's critics should object to his Dutch origins and cosmopolitan circle of advisers when Charles had made no attempt to conceal his indifference to the—Protestant—national interest. The enduring tradition of "radical patriotism" to which Defoe belonged is concisely defined by Linda Colley:

> As in the seventeenth century, militant Protestantism was a major, perhaps the major, characteristic [of English patriotism]. Catholicism was popularly associated with alien, absolutist regimes, with large standing armies and with individual penury.[40]

Colley points out that the eighteenth century saw a continued tendency to invoke the seventeenth-century "Norman yoke" theories which linked current fears of French dominance to the myths of Anglo-Saxon oppression during and after the Norman Conquest.

The True-Born Englishman belongs unmistakably to this Francophobic tradition, though it allows readers to draw their own parallels between the modern-day threat to national sovereignty from Bourbon ascendancy (Defoe is quite explicit here, naming his opponents as those "who, pretending to be Protestants, have all along endeavoured to reduce the liberties and religion of this nation into the hands of King *James* and his Popish powers" [A3v]) and the invasion of 1066. In Part One Defoe narrates England's history in terms of successive invasions but places by far the heaviest emphasis on the creation of an Anglo-Norman aristocracy. The "Tryanny [*sic*]" (7) of William I is implicitly compared to the benevolent reign of William III, and Defoe's language reflects his interpretation of the Conquest as a foreshadowing of modern French absolutism. He also bears out Hill's perception that royal absolutism was identified by the Stuarts' opponents with "subversion of the law which protected property."[41] Hill is referring to seventeenth-century Parliamentarians, but Defoe had inherited the myth of the Norman yoke from them. In *The True-Born Englishman* the Stuarts "have our Ships and Merchants bought and sold" (28), while William I is described as a ruthless usurper who should serve as a warning against English complacency in future times:

> The great Invading *Norman* let us know
> What Conquerors in After-Times might do.
> To ev'ry Musqueteer he brought to Town,
> He gave the Lands which never were his own.
> When first the *English* Crown he did obtain,
> He did not send his *Dutchmen* home again.
> No Reassumptions in his Reign were known,
> D'Avenant might there ha' let his Book alone.
> No Parliament his Army cou'd disband;
> *He rais'd no Money, for he pay'd in Land.*
> He gave his Legions their Eternal Station,
> And made them all Freeholders of the Nation.
> He Canton'd out the Country to his Men,
> And ev'ry Soldier was a Denizen.
> The Rascals thus Enrich'd, he called them *Lords*,
> To please their Upstart Pride with newmade Words,
> And *Doomsday Book* his Tryanny [*sic*] Records.   (6-7)

The description evokes Louis XIV no less than William I; Louis's territorial ambitions were at the heart of English Protestant anxieties about "Popery" as a threat to the "Balance of Europe," and Defoe is clearly arguing that the English should know what to expect from the

Continental descendants of the eleventh-century conqueror. The Davenant to whom he refers so sarcastically is not, of course, Sir William (1606-1668), but his son Charles (1656-1714), political economist and outspoken critic of various policies adopted by William III's Parliaments. In 1700 he had published a pamphlet entitled *A Discourse upon Grants and Resumptions; showing how our ancestors have proceeded with such ministers as have procured themselves grants of the crown-revenue; and that the forfeited estates ought to be applied towards the payment of public debts.* The thrust at Davenant is, then, intended as a rejoinder to yet another of William's critics.

Having explored Defoe's various polemical devices and strategies in *The True-Born Englishman,* particularly his appropriations of historical "facts" and national myths, we can see that far from a manifesto of tolerance, his poem is implacably Francophobic and anti-Catholic. While this may reflect a quite rational opposition to political and religious absolutism, the fact is that Defoe is adroit at exaggerating and manipulating the facts, and at deploying a number of what might be called nationalist fictions, including racist stereotypes. It is even difficult at times to know whether Defoe is rebutting the notion of a homogeneous English identity or iterating that we need to be on our guard against the loss of our heritage as a consequence of mass immigration: "We have been *Europe's* Sink, the *Jakes* where she / Voids all her Offal Outcast Progeny" (8). In fact Defoe is not anticipating Powellist incitements to racist hatred, since he clearly has no time for an ideology of ethnic "purity" (indeed those "Nations" [A2] which are pure, such as the Scots, Welsh and Irish, do not in his view gain thereby), but it would be fair to say that he is selectively opposed to immigration. Huguenots are welcome, as are other Continental and Scots Protestants ("*God, we thank thee!*—sent them hither" [8]), but only because they are allies against the Scottish Jacobites who came to England during the reign of James I and who are are, in contrast, exceedingly unwelcome:

> The Off-spring of this Miscellaneous Crowd
> Had not their new Plantations long enjoy'd,
> But they grew *Englishmen,* and rais'd their Votes,
> At Foreign Shoals for *Interloping Scots.* (8)

Given that *The True-Born Englishman* is as partial as its counterparts, such as Tutchin's *The Foreigners,* and just as dependent on nationalist rhetoric, it remains to be explained exactly how Defoe believed his position supported the English national interest, for, like many nationalists before and since, he fails to state this explicitly, and understanding it is obviously a key to the equivocations here and elsewhere in his work. The obliqueness which is characteristic of Defoe is, as we see from *The True-Born Englishman*, directly linked to his political convictions, for these required him to experiment endlessly with the rhetorical tools at his disposal.

I suspect that the reasons for supporting William and decrying the Stuarts were so familiar to Defoe and his readers that he felt little pressure to give them clear definition, but this is only partly adequate as an explanation for the apparent vacuum at the heart of *The True-Born Englishman*; after all, Defoe is not at all coy when it comes to certain clichés, such as the national blight of "Civil Feuds" (1); popery and "Wooden Shoes" (10); or the ancient rights of the British subject to depose a tyrannical king ("Englishmen *ha' done it many a time*" [21]). In 1701, the year of Defoe's poem, the Act of Settlement established the Protestant Succession; in the same year, the War of the Spanish Succession began. Both events highlighted the same issues which had been raised by the wars against France in the 1690s; significantly they also suggested the ambiguity surrounding William's motives. As Ogg explains:

> On 7 May William declared war on Louis, stating as his reasons that the latter had invaded the empire; he had encroached on the Newfoundland fisheries; he had invaded the Caribbean Islands and had seized New York and territory in Hudson's Bay; French privateers had attacked English ships; heavy duties had been imposed on English imports into France, and some imports had been prohibited altogether; the right of the flag had been disputed; English Protestant subjects had been persecuted in France. Here was a mixture of accusations, some unreasonable, and one, the allegation about the seizure of New York, obviously based on misinformation. The old pretext of the flag was now somewhat outworn; that Louis had invaded the empire was true, but that was not a serious English concern; and as for French tariffs, England also had her discriminations against foreign imports. There was some truth in the other accusations but, even taken together, they would hardly have justified war. Yet men are often most in the right when least able to explain themselves. England's motive was to preserve the Revolution settlement and keep out James II.[42]

At the risk of conflating the situation in 1690 with that in 1701, it would seem reasonable to extrapolate from this account an explanation for the haziness of Defoe's tribute to William in *The True-Born Englishman*. As Ogg implies, commercial and Protestant interests were inextricably intertwined, and many political observers, including Defoe, were hard put to articulate the relationship between them coherently.

Irrationality is, of course, at the heart of nationalism, and since Defoe's aim is the quintessentially nationalist one of valorising his king it comes as little surprise to find his poem fundamentally lacking in clarity. It begins as a statement on behalf of reason and enlightenment, its title parodying the very idea of true birth. But like the majority of liberal interventions in the debate over national identity, it is far from innocent of nationalist sentimentalism. In collapsing a favourite nationalist fiction, that of ethnic purity, Defoe is guided not by a boldly cosmopolitan tolerance but the very reverse, a compelling desire to safeguard English national identity as he conceived it. In rejecting racial purity and definitions based on geographical boundaries Defoe merely substitutes for them the equally contentious notion that true Englishness is an intangible essence of shared cultural values.

As we shall discover in subsequent chapters, the fundamental contradictions and weaknesses of his political beliefs, coupled with an unflagging determination to propagate them, are what Defoe's celebrated (and at times despised) juxtapositions of fact and fiction are designed to conceal and remedy. His palpable glee in 1707 when he wrote to tell Harley that his spying activities were producing results (quoted above, p. 9) is an indication of the strength of his desire for involvement in the world of public affairs. He sought throughout his life to take part in public events, resembling seventeenth- and eighteenth-century writers who combined their literary work with parliamentary, judicial or administrative careers, and it is an aspiration he shares with many of his fictional narrators. I have already suggested that the etymology of the other common term for spy, "agent," prompts us to consider Defoe's spying as a kind of activism which he more typically carried out by literary means, though, as with his spying, he conducted himself somewhat discreetly in his writings, or at least with "Mannagemt." To be sure, a dominant concern of Defoe's letters to Harley during his employment as a spy is the need for remuneration (e.g., "Thus Sir you have a Widdo' and Seaven Children On your hands"),[43] and certain of his methods suggest a willingness to use whatever means necessary to achieve his ends. Even so, his commitment to various causes and more importantly his conception of the writer as a practical agent of historical change suggest that his intentions were ultimately public-spirited, if at times self-deluding.

They also suggest some important lessons for ourselves, in an age when intellectuals and writers are increasingly polarized in opposition to the state, and increasingly impotent or unwilling to intervene (other than chorically) in political events. Defoe's vigorous grasp on the material realities of his society, witnessed most famously in Robinson Crusoe's dogged persistence in bread-making, is not a sign of myopic parochialism but the reverse: a symbol of his belief that a determined individual can make a tangible and significant contribution to his or her society.

CHAPTER ONE

Defoe's *Cavalier*:
Memoir or Memorandum?

Like the others in this book, this chapter focuses on a single text by Defoe and analyses its ideological functions as revealed by its historiography. *Captain Singleton*, I will argue, explores issues of political theory, while *Colonel Jack* foregrounds the processes by which history is constructed; *Moll Flanders* warns its readers about the rising crime wave, and *Robinson Crusoe* critiques the mania for speculation in overseas trading companies. Unlike any of these works, *Memoirs of a Cavalier*[1] purports to have been written long before the time of its publication, 1720, and offers itself as an innocuous personal memoir whose interest for the reader of the 1720s is purely antiquarian. But unsurprisingly, perhaps, given Defoe's zealous promotion of certain political, economic and social causes elsewhere in his work, *Memoirs of a Cavalier* is a deeply partisan re-envisioning of seventeenth-century history which has immediate relevance for his contemporaries.

Although set in the Europe of the Thirty Years War and the England of the Civil War, *Memoirs of a Cavalier* is intended as an oblique commentary on Hanoverian England and the Jacobite presence after 1715, and is a response to the perceived threat to Protestant Europe in the early decades of the eighteenth century from Bourbon ascendancy and the decline of the Swedish monarchy under Charles XII. It addresses political and religious issues crucial to England in 1720 and central to almost all Defoe's works: the evils of the Stuart cause; the virtues of the Glorious Revolution and the Act of Settlement; the dangers of Catholicism; the importance of Scotland for English affairs. In the title of this chapter, therefore, I have attempted to suggest a similarity between this text (an *apparently* neutral memoir or memorial of an individual's life) and the memorandum or informal diplomatic communication which is designed to convey a partisan assessment of events.

A major stumbling-block in the process of rescuing *Memoirs of a Cavalier* for modern readers is that it assumes a familiarity with seventeenth-century history. This is not to say that it aims at a learned audience—Defoe relies too heavily on plagiarising and borrowing from other well-known histories of the time such as Edmund Ludlow's *Memoirs*[2] and Bulstrode Whitelocke's *Memorials of the English Affairs*[3] to make that likely—or that it cannot be read from a standpoint of ignorance, but that it is a difficult book to assimilate and appreciate without a specific political context within which to judge it.

My main aim in what follows is to show the reasons for Defoe's consistently ironic and at times confusing portrayal of his narrator—reasons which are manifestly political—and to elucidate the ways in which his irony operates. There are very few passages, perhaps none at all, in *Memoirs of a Cavalier* which do not reflect and promote Defoe's political and sectarian interests in some way, often extremely ingeniously. What looks like a prolix, circumstantial, informal narrative is in fact an elaborately constructed and self-subverting representation of recent history: it is, literally, "cavalier" with the truth.

Like many Scots and Englishmen in the 1620s and 1630s, the unnamed Cavalier is drawn to events on the European Continent, eventually serving in the army of the Protestant Swedish king, Gustav II (referred to here, following Defoe, as Gustavus Adolphus), against the imperial forces of Austro-Hungary.[4] Part I of his narrative deals with Continental European history, Part II with his involvement in the English Civil War after his return. In both parts he is writing retrospectively, though his recall is detailed and apparently precise. The irony with which the reader is encouraged to regard him results from the unsuspecting frankness with which he reveals his self-interest in supporting Protestant and Stuart causes alike.

From the outset Defoe establishes his protagonist's credentials as a "typical" cavalier. We are told that the Cavalier chooses a military career partly because he is a cadet, or younger son, and that although he is relatively highly valued by his father as only the second son of his marriage, his status is ambiguous. Defoe is raising sensitive issues here: clearly his hero has an affinity with the monarch he will eventually serve in the English Civil War, for, as contemporaries would have been well aware, the Prince of Wales, the future Charles I, was likewise his father's second son, inheriting the throne only through the premature death of Prince Henry. In other respects too—his education and his favoured pursuits—the Cavalier's upbringing resembles that of the royal sons.

The discussion of the Cavalier's background is there to draw attention to the unjust and arbitrary nature of primogeniture and hence to allow Defoe to insinuate that the Stuarts' rule was unjust and arbitrary. Primogeniture reinforced the dynastic and patriarchal doctrines which were of intense concern to the Stuarts, as is clear from Charles I's stern advice to his youngest son, Henry Duke of Gloucester:

> he commanded him, upon his blessing, never to forget what he said to him upon this occasion, nor to accept or suffer himself to be made king whilst either of his elder brothers lived, in what part of the world soever they should be: that he should remember that the prince his brother was to succeed him by the laws of God and man; and if he should miscarry, that the duke of York was to succeed in the same right; and therefore that he should be sure never to be made use of to interrupt or disturb either of their rights; which would in the end turn to his own destruction.[5]

Charles sought to impress upon Henry the principle of hereditary kingship so cherished by his own father, James I, revealing the strong connection between royal authority and hierarchical notions of the family which would find its most notorious expression in Robert Filmer's *Patriarcha* (1638; pub. 1680) and its most eloquent critique in John Locke's first *Treatise of Government* (1690).[6]

Aside from raising the issue of primogeniture, Defoe is clearly concerned to portray the cultural and socio-economic background of a typical cavalier with accuracy. His protagonist is born in the county of Salop (Shropshire), a royalist stronghold, and is connected to a number of noble families in the area of Shrewsbury, whose castle will one day house the headquarters of Charles I. He casually mentions that he was born in Shrewsbury itself, Defoe apparently feeling it necessary to underline the association. The Cavalier's desire to become a soldier is a throwback to medieval feudalism, under which the aristocracy considered service to the king their most honourable course, though perhaps because he is a younger son the Cavalier will go abroad to fight.[7] To Defoe the problem is not that the Cavalier is a mercenary *per se*, but that he has no compunction in fighting for the reformed religion in Europe only to return to England to support a king whose Protestantism is highly dubious. The Cavalier indicts himself:

> I CONFESS, when I went into Arms at the Beginning of this War, I never troubled my self to examine Sides: I was glad to hear the Drums beat for Soldiers; as if I had been a meer *Swiss*, that had not car'd which Side went up or down, so I had my Pay. (125)

The reference is to the notoriously vacillating Swiss cantons, who changed sides between France and Spain largely according to the size of the retainers offered them. To Defoe in 1720, anxious to uphold the Protestant Succession and to identify patriotism with an unwavering

31

loyalty both to the reformed church and to the Hanoverians, the Cavalier is deplorably cynical. He is, of course, a virtual caricature of a royalist officer. After Oxford he spends his time hunting stags in the family woodlands, an activity which is as reminiscent of the violent disputes between landowners and tenants in the early 1720s as of seventeenth-century mores.[8] In keeping with this noble lifestyle, he has a marriage partner proposed to him, and a handsome settlement is offered.

The Cavalier has no wish to marry, so, like the contemporaneous and ill-fated match between the Prince of Wales and the Spanish Infanta (to which Defoe refers in an "editorial" footnote), this one is abandoned. His father's liberalism in this matter stands in direct opposition to the inflexibility which eventually spelt the Stuarts' downfall. The diplomatic clumsiness with which the match between the Prince of Wales and the Spanish Infanta was negotiated and then broken off contributed directly to that downfall, since it greatly increased the unpopularity of the king with the people.

In the "editorial" footnote (the Preface claims that the *Memoirs* derives from a hitherto lost manuscript by an anonymous gentleman, so the footnote is presumably intended to be understood as the work of whoever brought the text to light), Defoe refers explicitly to the most immediate consequences of the broken match: James I's withdrawal of support from the Protestant "Winter" King, Frederick of the Palatinate. James hoped to show good will towards Spain by abandoning Frederick, but to many English Protestants his actions were a betrayal of their religious allies and James's own daughter, the beautiful and popular Queen Elizabeth of Bohemia, Frederick's wife. Defoe includes the discussion between the Cavalier and his father (and its key) not only to raise the issue of arranged marriage but to remind his readers of the longstanding Catholic sympathies of the Stuarts. The Winter King whom James slighted was the grandfather of the future George I of England, the reigning monarch when *Memoirs of a Cavalier* was published.

Ignoring his father's mild objections, the Cavalier now sets off, as did so many wealthy young Englishmen in the seventeenth and eighteenth centuries, to complete his formal education with the Grand Tour; his companion is another younger son, a former college friend. From the first, the Cavalier rejects the conventional aims of travellers and the usual subjects of travel writing, showing no interest in the antiquities around which the Tour was traditionally arranged.[9] His interest in the immediate, mundane details of his narrative creates a naïvety of tone which helps to disguise Defoe's political sub-text. Part I of *Memoirs of a Cavalier* is not in fact a traveller's diary at all but a consciously slanted account of the Thirty Years War. It has not always been understood as such, however, since it proceeds largely by stealth. For example, a priest who gives the young Englishman some money when one of his horses is stolen is the occasion of an apparently innocent reflection on the covetousness of the French in general, and France gradually emerges in the *Memoirs* as a minefield for English travellers, the Cavalier suffering from disputatious customs-officers at the ports, horse-thieves on the roads, and pickpockets in the cities. Moreover, the "dextrous" tricks of France's petty thieves are not just evidence of Defoe's constitutional Francophobia; they are juxtaposed with, and implicitly compared to, the notoriously slippery statecraft of Cardinal Richelieu, who features extensively in Part I. As an opponent of French territorial ambition and as a Protestant, Defoe distrusted Richelieu, and he represents him as a consummately manipulative politician.

We catch frequent glimpses of Defoe's true attitudes and opinions behind the persona of his narrator. That the narrative's perspective, contrary to appearances, is distinctively English and, moreover, Protestant, is suggested in numerous ways. For example, as an Englishman the Cavalier finds he cannot evade the issue of the Huguenots (or French Protestants) of La Rochelle, whose cause was disastrously espoused by the Duke of Buckingham (the same Buckingham who had failed to secure the marriage of Prince Charles with the Spanish Infanta) and who were subsequently crushed by the French government. In the first of several asides the Cavalier blames his earlier ignorance of England's culpability in the affair on his youth, and reflects that he is now wiser as to the truth of the matter.

To convince the reader that France is a place of dishonesty and intrigue, Defoe next has the Cavalier relate a sensational incident in which he was mistakenly wounded by an unknown assailant whom he murders in a heated duel. The story bears no logical relation to the rest of the *Memoirs* and must therefore have been included for its bearing on the ethics of the French. Duelling is forbidden in France, whereas it persists in England, but the moral of the Cavalier's story is that the French are violent, arbitrary, and given to duelling in secret, where all kinds of chicanery are possible. Their ostensibly enlightened laws on duelling are not, therefore, preferable to the controversially permissive laws of the English.[10]

The Cavalier's effectiveness in conveying a sense of French society in the early 1630s depends on his facile combination of such small-scale episodes with general observations supposedly derived from his own experiences but in fact culled from standard histories of the period familiar to Defoe. At times the Cavalier's account echoes Jean Le Clerc's *Life of Richelieu*, for example, which was translated by Tom Brown and published in 1695.[11] He refers, as did Le Clerc, to the cries of the populace for cheaper bread and to their violence against the tax-collectors, most of whom had been appointed by Richelieu. As with the duelling incident this reference is included as much for its bearing on English history as for its local colour. The Queen Mother, Marie de' Medici, displays great courage and resolution in addressing her people and quelling the bread riots before they can spread, and the Cavalier compares her political skill with the ineptness of Charles I in the face of "popular Tumults" (21).

Even at this early stage of his *Memoirs* the Cavalier is exhibiting the suspect emotional detachment and lack of political commitment (or worse, a willingness to admire the French) which will be his hallmark. His ambivalence is not a source of irony for its own sake but a device which Defoe uses to undermine the ideological position of the English royalists, revealing its weaknesses and contradictions. If Marie de' Medici's statecraft is a paradigm with which Charles's incompetence contrasts strikingly, Richelieu and Louis XIII are also characterized by the Cavalier in terms that evoke an inevitable comparison with Charles I and his fatal malleability in the hands of Buckingham, Laud and others. The Cavalier does not draw the parallel directly, but Louis's domestic problems largely arise from the need to raise taxes for wars in which the populace have no interest, just as Parliament's confrontations with Charles stemmed principally from its resentment of Ship Money, a tax levied to support the navy at the (perceived) expense of the inland counties.

In order to move freely in wartime France the Cavalier and his friend adopt Scottish identities and carry the passes given to them by the Queen Mother. The reason for the pretence is that Scotland and France were informal allies, the Bourbons' somewhat lukewarm support for the Stuarts being a factor in Anglo-French relations throughout the mid- to late seventeenth century and on into the eighteenth. Since the Cavalier is an adherent of Charles Stuart anyway, it is ironic that this deceit is forced on him, but in 1630 English sympathy with the plight of the Huguenots was still causing friction between the English and French courts. For Defoe, France was a permanent enemy, and the Cavalier's exploitation of French pro-Scottish feeling is an unpleasant reminder that from 1688 onwards, as well as during the Commonwealth, France provided the exiled Stuarts with a home.

Though happy to avail himself of the Bourbons' protection, the Cavalier is wary of becoming involved in the war between France and Spain in Italy, which is a territorial conflict rather than a religious war. His hesitation seems to stem less from a philosophical objection to fighting alongside Catholics than from a practical cautiousness about joining an army of such "indifferent Troops" (22). He is hostile to the encroaching imperialists, Spain and Germany (23), but critical of the poor quality of the French soldiers. When he is finally unable to put off going into action his attitude is a combination of opportunism and fear, and like so many actual seventeenth-century soldiers he deserts at the first sign of real danger. The indiscipline of their armies, whether conscripted or professional, was a constant problem for generals in the period, both on the Continent and in the English Civil War.[12] As the Cavalier makes clear, an army containing diverse nationalities and new recruits was likely to disintegrate under fire:

> I run away very fairly one of the first, and my Companion with me, and by the Goodness of our Horses got out of the Fray, and being not much known in the Army, we came into the Camp an hour or two after, as if we had been only riding abroad for the Air. (24)

In emphasizing the unreliability of the seventeenth-century professional soldier Defoe is not merely reiterating a commonplace; he is also concerned to expose his protagonist's cowardice. In stressing the physical dangers of battle and the unheroic feelings of its participants he is no pacificist; he merely wants to show that the French were not half so powerful as they would like their English opponents to think. He recognizes that written histories were a valuable means of French self-aggrandizement; trumpeting seventeenth-century victories long after the event could intimidate contemporary enemies, and in 1720, it was well worth trying to set the record "straight."

Given the importance of documents in times of war—*Memoirs of a Cavalier* is full of letters, treaties, communications and written ultimata—and the ethical stress placed on the soldier's "word" (53), it is perhaps to be expected that the narrative displays a sensitivity to the powers of various texts, but Defoe's preoccupation with written (and verbal) representation is fundamental to his purposes. The historian may be as instrumental in shaping the course of events as the general or statesman, especially in war, when perceptions are heightened and confused. *Memoirs of a Cavalier* attacks histories of France which exaggerate its strength; histories of the Thirty Years War which obscure England's abandonment of her allies; and histories of the Civil War which exonerate Charles I. Defoe unabashedly proposes his own version of events as an alternative to these inadequate and misleading efforts by earlier historiographers.

Aside from attacking the French, the main purpose of Part I is, therefore, to commemorate Gustavus and to use him as a yardstick against which to measure England's leaders. English admiration for Gustavus Adolphus, the most vivid and successful defender of the Reformation in Europe, persisted throughout the seventeenth century and had been given fresh impetus in the eighteenth by the contrast with the failures of Gustavus's descendant, Charles XII of Sweden, against Peter the Great in the Northern Wars which began in 1700.[13]

In introducing the subject of Gustavus, Defoe's Cavalier recapitulates the background story of the war in Germany and in doing so exploits the opportunity to present the Swedish king as Protestant saviour. Though acknowledging that Gustavus was partly motivated by a private resentment of the Austro-Hungarian emperor's support of the Poles in Sweden's Polish war, the Cavalier is confident that the Swedish invasion of Austro-Hungary was chiefly instigated by the Protestant princes. His account of the Swedes' coercion of their reluctant allies is careful to exclude any reference to the fact that the German Protestants were quite naturally hostile towards what was, in the final analysis, a foreign aggressor. For the Cavalier there is no question about Gustavus's sincerity as Protestant champion; the German princes are simply unable to recognize their own best interests. That he is pressing a somewhat controversial point here is signalled by his self-conscious invocation of his own authority as a first-hand witness: "I have had some particular Opportunities to hear these Things from the Mouths of some of the very Princes themselves, and therefore am the forwarder to relate them" (38).

Throughout his detailed reconstruction of the Thirty Years War Defoe has his Cavalier frame his ostensibly eye-witness observations within a narrative which in fact clearly stems from a historical overview of the events he describes. His account is made all the more compelling because he appears to remain at only one remove from death and disaster, but the frequency of his lucky escapes signals the artifice of Defoe's historical reconstruction. At Torgau, for example, the Cavalier leaves just before the imperialists begin their seige, sketching the citizens' preparations with an eye for the captivating detail, but fleeing in time to continue his panoramic survey of the war. He is present at all the key moments: the fall of Magdeburg, the Battle of Breitenfeld, and the battle of the river Lech.

36

Though partisan, Defoe's description of Breitenfeld is accurate in all respects, being derived mainly from William Watts's *The Swedish Intelligencer* (1632-33), a contemporary news-book. Defoe's emphasis is on the tactical brilliance of the Swedish king, particularly in deploying his cavalry. In this he merely emphasizes what was historical fact: it was Gustavus's famous methods, based on those of Maurice, Prince of Orange, of using his cavalry, infantry and pikemen in combination which made him so invincible in the minds of his contemporaries.[14] The Swedish army was also celebrated for its discipline in the aftermath of battle, and the Cavalier is careful to point out that Gustavus permitted the enemy to be plundered only after the field had been cleared of the wounded. Nonetheless, Defoe's partisan viewpoint is obvious, and his readers were meant to draw an inevitable comparison between this policy and the legendary atrocities of the royalists in the English Civil War. Moreover, Defoe's admiration for the democratic temperament and meritocratic principles of Gustavus is held in tension with the Cavalier's own affinity with traditional hierarchies of king and knight, father and son, land-owner and tenant. Defoe makes a two-pronged attack on cavalier ideology here: Gustavus is praised for his professional efficiency, and the Cavalier is used to hint at the weaknesses of a system based on outmoded feudal values.

Towards the end of the Cavalier's European travels Frederick of Bohemia arrives from England, where he has been cooling his heels in exile, unable to obtain the backing of the Stuarts, his wife's family. He is accompanied by a corps of Dutch cavalrymen and English gentlemen whose patriotism stands in shameful contrast to the betrayal of their cause by both James and Charles. The Cavalier is proud to be reminded that his own father served more than thirty years ago under the Protestant Prince Maurice of Orange in the Dutch-Spanish war, distinguishing himself at the Battle of Nieupoort (July 1600). The reference to Maurice is important, since it is proleptic of William III, the son of William II and Maurice's grandson, and suggests a line of Anglo-Dutch Protestant champions who are akin to Gustavus in their courage and determination to uphold the Reformation. Defoe's personal and philosophical commitment to William III is evident in many of his works, even those written long after William's death,[15] and *Memoirs of a Cavalier* may be read as a veiled celebration of his military exploits in the Low Countries in the 1690s as well as a tribute to Gustavus Adolphus's achievements in Germany sixty years later.

Defoe structures Part I of the Cavalier's narrative so that it loosely resembles a classical tragedy of which Gustavus Adolphus is the hero. Up to this point Gustavus has swept across Germany virtually unhindered, and is at the pinnacle of his success when he faces the imperial generalissimo Wallenstein at Nuremberg in the summer of 1632. Wallenstein was perhaps the most formidable and legendary of all the imperial commanders of the Thirty Years War. Unlike Gustavus, he habitually allowed his troops to plunder indiscriminately as they went, a policy which would ultimately debilitate the empire and contribute to Ferdinand's defeat. But in the early 1630s Wallenstein was in the ascendancy, arguably more powerful than the emperor himself, since only he could afford to maintain the huge armies protecting the imperialists from the Protestants.

Gustavus is at the height of his success just before his tragic death. The Cavalier gives an exhaustive account of Nuremberg's efficient internal organization under the seige, and an equally detailed description of Gustavus's encampment beyond it. Seventeenth-century encampments were frequently built on an immense scale, with fortification lines more than twenty miles long and high escarpments; creating and maintaining such earthworks was what made seiges so expensive. The encampment at Nuremberg is both huge and elaborate, yet Gustavus has not had to give up the offensive by deploying too many men there since three allied forces remain at large, commanded by Gustavus Horn, Oxenstierna, and two of the Protestant electors, respectively. Paralleling the growing stature of Gustavus throughout Part I, Defoe's Cavalier has become increasingly important to his commander. During the seige he is required to storm a garrison which yields enormous quantities of booty and which consolidates Gustavus's grip on the province. However, in one skirmish he is forced into a humiliating retreat, and this and subsequent failures seem to anticipate the critical downturn in Swedish fortunes after Gustavus falls in battle. The Cavalier is taken prisoner at this point, and his passionate concern for the progress of the war declines from the death of Gustavus onwards. He justifies his perfunctory account of the battle of Lutzen (November 1632) by the fact that he was absent from it himself, but he is clearly numb with grief at the loss of the king. Modern historians bear out Defoe's description of Protestant Germany's overwhelming sense of loss when their champion was slain, though it has also been suggested that the news was a relief to some who were beginning to feel that Gustavus was a conqueror not only of the imperialists but of the empire itself.

Released from imprisonment in Leipzig, the Cavalier has no stomach for more fighting, and sensing that with the loss of Gustavus the war has entered a new phase he turns from active service to the world of the generals, and becomes a close adviser to those who assume military command in Gustavus's place. His previous association with the king is the reason for this privileged position, he modestly explains, though he remains rather distant from the new commanders and has no compunction in declaring that, along with Gustavus Horn, he was totally opposed to fighting the disastrous Battle of Nordlingen, the first serious allied defeat since Sweden's invasion. He also claims to have seen from the outset that the battle plan drawn up by the generals was deeply flawed.

The themes of the first part of the narrative are further developed in the second, which deals chiefly with the English Civil War and which draws parallels between English and Continental history. As Part II makes clear, the Cavalier's attitude to battle is at a considerable remove from the traditional, simple and amateurly belief that sheer courage and physical endurance are guarantors of success. The misguided enthusiasts who rush into battle without pausing to consider strategy— Duke Bernard at Nordlingen, for instance, or Prince Rupert at Edgehill—are far less admired by the Cavalier than the more cautious and cerebral professional soldiers—Gustavus Adolphus, Gustavus Horn, Sir Thomas Fairfax—who stop to think before charging into danger. Defoe's point is that modern, professional soldiery is superior to the courtly ideal of knighthood which values derring-do above subtle tactics. In Part II the English royalists are repeatedly portrayed as rash, even foolhardy, in combat, while, like Gustavus, the more level-headed parliamentarians will not allow themselves to be carried away in the heat of battle.

Suggestive parallels are frequently drawn between events in England and those on the Continent in Part II. The Cavalier has no interest in the religious issues which are at the heart of the conflict between the Scots and the king, and the striking contrast with his previous stout loyalty to the Protestant cause on the Continent indicates that Defoe intended him to symbolize the royalists' position in the 1630s—in short, vapid and lacking in conviction. Towards the end of Part I the Cavalier appears to support the king out of nothing more than dumb loyalty: "I was ready to serve him against any that his Majesty thought fit to account his Enemies, and should count it an Honour to receive his Commands" (122), he says lamely.

Yet if the Cavalier's devotion to the king's cause evidently lacks philosophical justification, it nonetheless seems preferable to the apathy that the Scottish rebellion inspires in most English minds. The king has difficulty constituting even two regiments; the rest of his army is made up of private regiments commanded by individual noblemen. Once able to raise five troops of men to fight for Gustavus in Germany, the Cavalier can now find only eight gentlemen and thirty-six "Countrymen" (farmers or yeomen) willing to serve King Charles. As he bitterly remarks, even these few are superfluous, since the king commits the classic error of becoming entrenched (an error never committed by Gustavus, we remember); as a result, there is no decisive battle, and valuable resources are consumed to no purpose.

Scottish loyalties were by no means homogeneous in the period 1639-60, which helps to explain the apparent contradictions in Defoe's narrator. Like a true cavalier he condemns the Covenanters for joining with Parliament in the first place and for surrendering the king in January 1647, yet he later admires Montrose as "a gallant daring Soldier" (249). Such is his contempt for the Engagers, whom he regards as entirely self-interested (266-67), that he makes no reference whatever to Hamilton's invasion, which took place while the king was on the Isle of Wight. There are hints, however, that Defoe himself was not so unforgiving towards the Scots, for the beginning of Part II refers to their oppression in 1638-39 (134), while their sufferings during the war are mentioned towards the end (255).[16]

The reader becomes increasingly aware of the Cavalier as a sophisticated narrative device whereby Defoe is able to criticize the royalist forces apparently from the viewpoint of an insider. Even during the inconclusive confrontation in Northumberland (123) he is disgusted by his fellows. He finds them more eager to "devour" the countryside than defend their monarch, and given to costly displays which raise doubts about their future competence in battle. He objects to their disregard for traditional social hierarchies, and scorns the footmen and servants with whom the noblemen have filled their troops. He is also contemptuous of the "Crouds of Parsons" (123) who surround the king and provoke resentments in those nobles who should have been most zealous in the cause. The king himself is an elusive figure in the Cavalier's account. Though it is Charles who summons a Council of War at Berwick, the near-fatal decision to send the Earl of Holland on a reconnaissance mission is taken collectively, suggesting a leadership vacuum. Only the cowardice or folly of the enemy saves the king from premature outright defeat, in the Cavalier's view.

Part II, then, is intimately bound up in ideological terms with Part I, even though the subject-matters of the sections are so different. It may be conjectured that Defoe juxtaposes the Thirty Years War and the English Civil War in order to reveal the inadequacy of the Stuart kings by contrast with Gustavus and, conversely, to uphold by implication the Revolution Settlement and the Hanoverian Succession respectively as signs of Protestantism's ultimate triumph in Britain over monarchical and religious absolutism. The contrast between the Cavalier's honourable European service and his rather less admirable reasons for joining the inadequate forces of Charles I on his return to England is intended, at least in part, to reflect the inconsistency and incoherence of the cavaliers' ideological position as Defoe saw it.

There is a further reason for the narrative's bipartite structure. At the beginning of Part II the Cavalier wonders why, given his knowledge of Germany's devastation, he had nevertheless gloated in 1639 over the prospect of war in his native country. Defoe's implication is that war is contagious; exposed to battle in Europe, the Cavalier and many others like him had become infected by it. Modern historians such as Geoffrey Parker have debated whether or not there was a "general crisis" in seventeenth-century Europe and have found evidence for both contemporary and eighteenth-century beliefs that a massive upheaval did take place across the Continent in the period, though neither early nor modern commentators are agreed as to its causes or extent. Parker cites Jeremiah Whittaker preaching to the Commons; John Goodwin, the parliamentary pamphleteer; John Milton; Ralph Josselin, clergyman; Robert Mentet de Salmonet; and Thomas Hobbes—all of whom posited a pan-European crisis manifested chiefly in popular (often violent) challenges to existing constitutions.[17] In the mid-eighteenth century Voltaire wrote his *Essais sur les moeurs et l'esprit des nations* (1741-42; published 1756), after which the notion of a "general crisis" in the seventeenth century was increasingly adopted by historians.

Memoirs of a Cavalier has not previously received attention in these debates as to whether there really was a seventeenth-century crisis and whether contemporary and early eighteenth-century commentators believed that there was one, yet Defoe's narrative is shaped by the fundamental assumption that events in Europe and England are interrelated. As far as the the Cavalier is concerned the English are simply too keen to follow the bloody example of the imperialists, but for Defoe the analogy has other important ramifications. Read as a critique not so much of war but of unjust war, his *Memoirs* are a lament for England's neglect of the Reformation at a time when heroic sacrifices were being made for it in Sweden, Germany and Scotland; it is a lament, too, for the errors of the Stuarts; and for the vanity of the royalists who fought, according to the Cavalier, without principle or distinction for a justly doomed cause. Whereas the Thirty Years War ended with the Peace of Westphalia, "which has since been the Foundation of the *Protestants* Liberty, and the best Security of the whole Empire" (113), the English Civil War ended in nihilism:

> I always expected that in a Chain of Distractions, as it generally fals out, the last Link would be Destruction; and though I pretended to no Prophecy, yet the Progress of Affairs have brought it to pass, and I have seen Providence, who suffered, for the Correction of this Nation, the Sword to govern and devour us, has at last brought Destruction *by the Sword*, upon the Head of most of the Party who first drew it. (270)

That the Cavalier has found himself for the first time on the wrong side is implicit throughout Part II. When he sees the Scottish infantry moving alongside and intermingled with their horse, he is irresistibly reminded of Gustavus's simultaneous deployment of all three instruments at his disposal: musketry, cavalry and pikes. His tone modulates to a nostalgic affection which betrays where his true loyalties lie:

> When I saw the Foot thus interlined among the Horse, together with the Way of ordering their flying Parties, it presently occurred to my Mind, that here was some of our old *Scots*, come home out of *Germany*, that had the ordering of Matters; and if so, I knew we were not a Match for them. (130)

As far as he is concerned, the conflict in Scotland is directly analogous to those on the Continent.

The reader may wonder how Defoe contrives to criticize the king's supporters without undermining the credibility of his royalist narrator. Though he remains on the side of the king, the Cavalier's analysis of the causes of the war is identical with the opposition's view that Charles used the (finite) resources of the treasury to avoid summoning a Parliament and that Archbishop Laud's highhandedness in Scotland provoked the rebellion there. He is not, however, a roundhead in disguise. To be sure, his discussion of the king's character is founded on the belief in his reliance on "evil Counsellors" (142) which characterized parliamentarian discourse before and during the war, and which was proclaimed in the Nineteen Propositions for reform presented to Charles on 1 June 1642.[18] But in keeping with his professed loyalty to the king the Cavalier regards royal "Obstinacy" as "An impolitic honesty" (137), and he evokes the image of a king seduced from his faithful nobles by artful priests. These nobles are both personally and ideologically committed to him, in contrast with the volatile and seditious Commons and such bewilderingly incompetent advisers as Stafford. Though the calling of Parliament is essential, it is an "unhappy Necessity" according to the

Cavalier, who has the conventional royalist resentment of an autonomous Commons.

Just as he was privy in Part I to the debates among European statesmen over the peace negotiations, so in Part II he finds himself at the heart of public affairs. Somewhat improbably he is both the confidant of Scottish ministers and the king's principal ambassador to Scotland. His political dexterity seems to indicate not so much a ruthless devotion to the king's cause as a fundamental lack of conviction. There were many moderate parliamentarians in the early 1640s who would have agreed with him that

> Had the House only regulated the Abuses of the Court, punished evil Counsellors, and restor'd Parliaments to their original and just Powers, all had been well; and the King, tho' he had been more than mortified, had yet reaped the Benefit of future Peace. (142)

In fact Part II is largely based on the memoirs of the republican, Edmund Ludlow, and is designed as well to undermine the standard royalist historiography articulated most famously in Clarendon's *History of the Rebellion*. *Memoirs of a Cavalier* lays bare many of the contradictions and evasions that Whig readers found in Clarendon's supposedly disinterested narrative. Thus, while Defoe's title implies that this text will be a royalist corrective to Ludlow's account both of cavalier war atrocities and conscientious parliamentarian attempts to formulate a constitutional settlement, his Cavalier cannot justify the shedding of blood on the king's behalf, or excuse the king's political inadequacies.

At the outset, Defoe has the Cavalier stress that the king had all the advantages on his side: the cream of the nobility;[19] grants equal to those of Parliament; widespread provincial support.[20] But he throws all these advantages away by an unprecedented reliance on fighting in the field, a tactic which admittedly speeds the progress of the war but which exhausts his armies and prevents them from consolidating their gains: "had the King fought less he had gained more" (151), says the Cavalier. Although he seems equally keen to criticize the strategies of the enemy, most of his remarks concerning the parliamentarians' errors are in fact designed to highlight his own side's failures to capitalize on them.

At Edgehill (23 October 1642), for example, even the parliamentarians' abject weariness does not permit the royalists a victory, initial success being negated by Prince Rupert's ill-considered pursuit of the fleeing enemy cavalry. And the Cavalier acknowledges that the conduct of Prince Rupert's troops is less than exemplary; they appear to be more interested in plunder than with defending their comrades. When one cavalier accuses Rupert's men of this, Rupert's intemperate response suggests that for Defoe he represents an aspect of Charles which contributes to his downfall: his imperious disregard for the proper forms of government. The parallel is suggested in the Cavalier's punning description of Rupert's haughty behaviour, which reflects as much on Charles's insistence on the royal prerogative as on Rupert himself: "The Prince was exceedingly provoked, and as he was very passionate, began to talk very oddly, and without all *Government of himself*" (161; emphasis added).[21]

After Edgehill, the Cavalier's resolve begins to falter, and Defoe's covert sympathy for the king's opponents is evident in his narrator's growing repugnance towards the horrors of an internecine war on his native soil. The Cavalier joins the parliamentarians in urging the king to make peace. As in Part I, when the Cavalier fought out of personal devotion to Gustavus rather than out of confessional zeal, Defoe is careful not to identify his protagonist too strongly with a particular church party ("I confess I had not much Religion in me, at that time" [165]), presumably because to do so might have been to destroy the mask concealing his true identity. Defoe does, however, allow the Cavalier to articulate sentiments which suggest a latitudinarian Anglicanism hostile to the episcopacy as well as to the radical Independents in the parliamentary army. Politically, too, the Cavalier is still at heart a moderate, hopeful of a restoration yet in favour of the "Constitution of Government" as represented by Parliament. Edgehill, to the Cavalier, is an appropriate moment to break off hostilities, leaving both the king and Commons with incentives to negotiate, not the least of which is the discovery that civil war is intolerably brutal and destructive.

Again it is Prince Rupert who destroys the hope of peace. His cavalrymen are descending helter-skelter on local neighbourhoods, collecting booty and commiting atrocities—actions that play into the hands of parliamentarian propagandists. Here again Defoe exploits the possibilities of the pseudo-autobiography with typical adroitness: his Cavalier is both present during these sorties, and thus qualified to describe them, but is also an apparently objective critic of them. In fact he is just the sort of gentleman volunteer to blame for the reputation acquired by the king's army even if, in attempting to exonerate Charles, he also tries to distance himself from the atrocities:

> 'Tis true, the King, who naturally abhorred such things, could not restrain his Men, no nor his Generals, so absolutely as he would have done. The War, on his Side, was very much *a al Voluntier*; many Gentlemen served him at their

own Charge . . . and this obliged him to wink at their Excursions upon the Country. (167-68)

The anecdote he relates about a party of carousing cavaliers who find themselves bested by a woman parliamentarian is an indication of the level of indiscipline to which the king's supporters have now fallen. For all the Cavalier's attempts to excuse his side, his obvious enjoyment of the story suggests a less than wholehearted admiration for some of his co-fighters: "a Troop of Women might have beaten them all" (170).

The Cavalier's account of the war after the winter of 1642-43 is on the face of it purely factual, including descriptions of both successes and defeats for the king. Yet the increasingly republican slant of his narrative is noticeable. Firstly he omits to record the death of the leading parliamentarian, John Hampden, at the Battle of Chalgrove Field on 18 June 1643. The loss of Hampden was a severe blow for the parliamentary side and it is significant, therefore, that Defoe ignores it. Second, and more important, the Cavalier repeatedly emphasizes the advantages enjoyed by the king's army, their huge resources brought from Europe by Queen Henrietta Maria, and the ease of their victories. While the confidence of the Cavalier—"this was the entire Destruction of their Army" (178)—is at first glance impressive, it ultimately begs the humiliating question why, despite winning so many battles, the cavaliers lost the war.[22] And third, the Cavalier recalls that it was during this critical period that Oliver Cromwell first began to impinge on the public consciousness.

Defoe's metaphor for the future Lord Protector—"who, like a little Cloud, rose out of the East" (186)—is not entirely original; similar figures are used by Clarendon (2:346-47) and Ludlow (1:98-99), for example. But the sudden and brief transposition to a poetic mode is an appropriate way to mark this most crucial of turning-points in the history of the war. Generally speaking, Defoe is less given to vivid detail than are actual histories; Ludlow, by contrast, relishes odd digressions into the circumstantial, as when he notes that he thwarted a royalist attempt to send his own father's provisions to the king, "amongst which there was half a dozen pasties of my father's venison ready baked" (1:53). When Defoe's Cavalier describes Cromwell the change is striking, recalling his awed references to Gustavus Adolphus in Part I: "Victory attended him like a Page of Honour," for example (187). As he explains, Cromwell's astonishing generalship more than compensated for the debilitated state of the parliamentary army, especially since the army was allowed to recoup while the royalists camped outside Gloucester.

In Defoe's description of the gruelling and increasingly desperate search for a safe haven by the Cavalier and his friends after Marston Moor (1644) there are echoes of the story of the fugitive Prince of Wales, the future Charles II, who escaped to the Continent after the Battle of Worcester in 1651. The prince made a six-week journey across open countryside and through dense woodlands, and Clarendon made much of his Christ-like sufferings: "his feet, with the thorns in getting over hedges, and with the stones in other places, were so hurt and wounded, that he many times cast himself upon the ground" (5:217). Like Charles II the Cavalier's party is forced to hide in a wood and travel in disguise, but Defoe's tone is quite different from Clarendon's. The once heroic officers of the king are reduced to dressing up like stage rustics, and there is comedy in the Cavalier's boast that "My pretended Country Woman acted her Part to the Life, though the Party was a Gentleman of good Quality of the Earl of *Worcester*'s family" (207). Comedy degenerates into farce when the Cavalier is challenged by a group of genuine "Clowns" (209) who correctly suspect he has stolen their horse.[23]

The royalists' defeats, however, have personal reverberations for the Cavalier, whose own father is a prisoner at Shrewsbury. The family silver has largely gone to support the king, and now the parliamentarians seem poised to confiscate their woodlands. Although the Cavalier does not explicitly contrast his circumstances with those of Rupert, there was considerable resentment of Rupert's disregard for English life and property, as illustrated by the chants of the people of Bristol as he surrendered to Fairfax: "Give him no quarter, give him no quarter."[24]

As on previous occasions, the Cavalier wholly fails to provide a convincing defence of the king's conduct at the end of the war. He chooses to ignore rather than try to refute the reasons for the Presbyterians' grievances, for example, and his justification of the appalling atrocities committed by the besiegers at Leicester is patently flawed by self-contradictions. At first he claims the authority of an eye-witness, but an inadvertent slip ("I caused my Men to attack it" [242]) soon shows that far from being a mere witness, or even a participant, he actually instigated the slaughter of civilians in their homes. By once again allowing him both to criticize royalist errors and contribute to them, Defoe undermines his credibility as an apologist for the king's side.

The effect of Defoe's emphasis on his narrator's venality compromises the judgments of the Cavalier himself as a historiographer, but more importantly it calls into question the collective principles, if any, of the royalists. As subsequent chapters will confirm, one of Defoe's most characteristic procedures was to encourage the reader's doubts about his protagonists' trustworthiness, and his aim was always ideological. *Colonel Jack*, for example, is an exercise in sustained irony which prompts the reader's gradual recognition of Jack's infidelity to historical truth, while Moll Flanders's dishonesty extends from her life to her narration of it. In *Memoirs of a Cavalier* signs of the Cavalier's fundamental dishonesty are intended to induce a sceptical reassessment of the principles of honour central to royalist ideology and, as I have suggested, an equally sceptical response to royalist historiography.

Not surprisingly, given Defoe's antipathy to the Stuarts, his Cavalier refuses to echo traditional hagiographies of Charles as a noble martyr,[25] simply remarking that the army "sacrificed their King, and shed the Blood of the *English* Nobility without Mercy" (270). It is as though Defoe wishes to avoid explicit commentary on these events; his narrator simply refers the reader to other histories. The manoeuvre is a clever one, because it would have been almost impossible to maintain the fiction of a cavalier narrator whilst failing to echo traditional royalist laments for a wronged king.

Part I of *Memoirs of a Cavalier* ends with the fall of Gustavus Adolphus, Part II with that of Charles II. Historically, Gustavus's death in fact seemed to mark the end of the Reformation in Europe, yet the Peace of Westphalia, as the Cavalier frequently reminds us, was in sight, and Charles's execution too has unspoken advantages for the Protestant cause. In its formal symmetry *Memoirs of a Cavalier* places the English Civil War in a pan-European debate between Catholic and Protestant, monarchist and republican, church and state.

It also explores the causal link between the Continental wars and the English Civil War for, as Defoe hints, the disastrous foreign policies of the early Stuarts were a major factor in the deterioration of the relationship between Crown and Commons. To begin with, there were James I's attempts to forge an alliance with Spain, a country detested by the English people for historical and religious reasons. When the Commons finally succeeded in persuading Charles I to send a naval expedition under the Duke of Buckingham to Cadiz in 1625, the results were disastrous and provoked recriminations between the king and Parliament which lasted until 1628. Defoe's Cavalier alludes directly to the conflicting interests of the anti-Spanish Commons and the pro-Spanish king when he remembers his father speculating about the possibility of a war with Spain (10).

According to the internal chronology of the *Memoirs* this conversation took place in 1628-29, just before the Cavalier went to Europe in the spring of 1630. As the recent editor of the *Memoirs* observes, it is difficult to know of what war the Cavalier's father is supposed to be speaking, since England and Spain were in fact already at war at that time (300 n. 4). An explanation is found in Defoe's preoccupation with the tensions between monarch and people throughout the *Memoirs*. He was less interested in factual accuracy than in reminding the reader that in the 1620s the Stuarts were sympathetic to Spain. It is significant that he chooses to ignore the expedition to Cadiz which, though itself unpopular, did at least show Charles prepared to satisfy Parliament's demands for an aggressively anti-Spanish policy.

In a footnote to the same conversation, Defoe (in editorial guise) refers to the policy of the king with regard to the "old Quarrel" between Bohemia and the Elector Palatine. James had outraged English Protestant opinion with his refusal to commit forces to restore Frederick after the imperial counter-invasion of Bohemia, and Charles had been no more successful, though he was more willing, in his attempts to protect his sister and brother-in-law. Defoe does not draw an explicit parallel between events in Bohemia, where a Protestant uprising led to the deposition of a Catholic monarch, and events in England after 1642, but the *Memoirs* as a whole is designed to highlight the contrasts between the Protestant kings of Europe and the unpopular, supposedly anti-Protestant kings of England. When James received Frederick's envoy he greeted him with a characteristic assertion of absolutism: "So now you are of the opinion that subjects can dispossess their kings? You are come in good time to England, to spread these principles among the people, that my subjects may drive me away, and place another in my room?"[26]

In addition to these references to Stuart foreign policy the Cavalier broods on the implications of La Rochelle for England's commitment to the Protestant cause (15-16), and makes scathing references to Spanish ambitions in Mantua (23); these firmly align him with the Commons regarding Anglo-Spanish relations. He is also plainly pro-Dutch, in contrast to James (who hoped to support Spain in the Netherlands), as evinced by his admiration for the "wonderful Power of Art" (119) of the Dutch military machine. These divergences from Stuart diplomatic thinking in Part I are paralleled by the hostility, just detectable, towards Queen Henrietta Maria in Part II, whom the Cavalier discovers fundraising "among her own Friends" (i.e., in France) in the early stages of the war.

Academic history did not interest Defoe; for him historical parallels were rhetorical tools with which to construct a compelling argument for the present political moment. In 1720 it was by no means obvious that the Hanoverian Succession was guaranteed or that the Protestant future of northern Europe was assured. The Jacobite threat had been renewed by the failed uprising of 1715, and in 1718 Charles XII of Sweden, dismal successor to a long line of Protestant champions, had been killed in battle. *Memoirs of a Cavalier* sets out to vindicate the Revolution Settlement of 1688 and the Hanoverian Succession which followed. It commemorates Gustavus Adolphus and thereby indirectly extolls his "natural" heirs William III and George I, and it exposes the insincerity, irresolution and ineffectiveness of the Stuarts and their Continental counterparts, the imperialists. Though it purports to be the reflections of a cavalier, the *Memoirs* record firstly, the stupendous achievements of the Swedish king and the barbarity of his Catholic enemies, and then the failures of the English royalist forces and the justness of parliamentary opposition to the royal prerogative. Underpinning this antithesis is the contrast between the professionalized and highly-disciplined army led by Gustavus and the feebleness of Charles's cavaliers, whose blind feudal loyalties are unsupported by any military experience or expertise, and who prove no match for the well trained New Model Army of Oliver Cromwell.

In *Memoirs of a Cavalier*, as in so many of his writings, Defoe celebrates Protestant will-power and refuses to reduplicate royalist hagiographies of Charles as religious martyr and patriot. He bases his story on republican accounts, pre-eminently those of Bulstrode Whitelocke and Edmund Ludlow. Yet superficially there seems no doubt about his narrator's familial, geographical and aristocratic affinities with the Stuart cause. He is born in a staunchly royalist county; his father has long-standing connections with the court; his innate sympathies are with the landed nobility in their conflict with the Commons. Defoe's strategy is subtle and persuasive: by portraying the typical cavalier from within (or apparently from within) he is able to show the adherents of the Stuart cause as lacking both in moral conviction and military competence. The Cavalier does his best to defend his king both in words and deed, but can do neither effectively. The inference cannot be mistaken: cavaliers, and hence Jacobites, are unsuccessful in the field and muddle-headed in their politics. In both Part I and Part II it is only the Protestant cause which inspires its followers and which boasts an unstoppable military machine.

Defoe recognizes that history can never be the merely objective rendering of empirical data; it is always a re-working of old arguments for contemporary debates. His Cavalier constantly pictures himself at the right hand of some great statesman or general, offering quiet but penetrating insights into their problems. Despite his high profile in the military sphere his methods of influencing events are often, therefore, covert and unofficial. In this they resemble the methods of Defoe himself, who seeks an inconspicuous, unexceptionable means of refuting the absolutist arguments of the Jacobites, the Tory inheritors of the Cavalier tradition, by showing through a quasi-autobiographical narrative that the origins of this tradition were anything but noble. Figuratively Defoe sits at the side of the perplexed observers of contemporary politics and provides them with a bird's-eye view. History for Defoe is not a passive subject for retrospective investigation; it is the means of influencing public life in the here and now. His Cavalier's *Memoirs* are the reverse of what they seem, a reverential memorial; in fact they overwhelmingly evoke the alternative meaning of the word "memoir," "memorandum," with all its connotations of a calculated political communication.

CHAPTER TWO

"I was . . . bold and wicked while I was under Government": Political theory in *Captain Singleton*

Almost twenty years after the publication of *The True-Born Englishman* (discussed in the Introduction) we find Defoe pursuing arguments almost identical to those of his signature poem, though his methods are now, like those in *Memoirs of a Cavalier* (1719), less direct. *Captain Singleton* (1720) [1] is, among other things, a consideration of the conflict between absolutism and contractual monarchy which *The True-Born Englishman* had sought to resolve in William's favour a generation before, and which had underpinned *Memoirs of a Cavalier*. Like the *Memoirs*, *Captain Singleton* is covert and at times almost obscure in its rhetorical strategies, which accounts for the fact that (again unlike the poem) it has only rarely been interpreted as a response to contemporary political struggles, and has more often been discussed in terms of its sources, whether ethnographical,[2] geographical,[3] or biographical.[4]

When, as with J. R. Moore, the critic has gone beyond the literary influences on the book, the emphasis has been on its affinities with Defoe's other writings on trade, especially *The General History of Discoveries and Improvements in Useful Arts* (1725-26) and *A Plan of the English Commerce* (1728), or his works on piracy such as *The King of Pirates* (1720), issues of *The Review* (1707) and, possibly, *A General History of the Pyrates* (1724).[5] One commentator does make his central concern the dialogue with theories of government in *Captain Singleton*, but even here the stated intention is to defend the thematic and structural coherence of the narrative against those who have dismissed it as chaotic and rambling.[6] The charge of rambling is, however, accurate—the novel is, after all, the account of a peregrination—and, if not chaotic, it is hardly systematic in its treatment of any subject, least of all political philosophy. Nonetheless, it is deeply imbued with Defoe's views of the relationship between the individual and the state, and although such views are relatively straightforward and little refined, their coded expression in a narrative which purports to be innocent of any tendentiousness is intriguing, and deserves analysis.

While this is my concern in this chapter, it should be stressed that *Captain Singleton* is not the kind of thinly disguised satire which hinges on loaded parallels with English society. Jonathan Swift's *Gulliver's Travels* (1722) is only the most famous and sustained of such (pseudo-) travel tales; among others, Mary Delarivier Manley's *New Atalantis* (1709) was well known in its own time for its cryptic libels of prominent Whigs. As Maximillian E. Novak points out, Defoe's own *Consolidator* (1705) is "a thinly disguised political satire in the form of an imaginary voyage."[7] By comparison with these texts, *Captain Singleton*'s frame of contemporary reference is minimal, its sideswipes at English culture and politics rarely specific.

Admittedly, at one point Singleton confesses he is something of a "projector," and so Defoe raises certain questions about the ethics of real-life projectors in early Hanoverian England. At another, the Captain draws wry analogies between pirates and supposedly legitimate merchants, a joke also used in *The Review*[8] and *The General History of the Pyrates*.[9] On the whole, however, the novel communicates a genuine interest in the exotic places and foreign people it describes, and in this sense belongs to the tradition of the "Strange but true" narrative, a subgenre which J. Paul Hunter attributes to the "rhetoric of desire" constructed by popular journalists such as John Dunton. This rhetoric was in turn a product of two cultural forces: the ascendancy of empiricism in early modern Europe, and the emphasis on interpretation which is "the essence of Protestantism."[10] *Captain Singleton* includes two digressions (111, 158-60), the meticulous detail of which is typically Defovean, and recalls nothing so clearly as the purification with vinegar of the infected coins in *A Journal of the Plague Year* (1722)[11] or the famously painstaking production of a loaf of bread in *Robinson Crusoe*. Equally indulgent of the naïvely curious reader is the description of the castaways' journey across the African interior, though in this section of the narrative Defoe is careful to avoid that plausible circumstantiality he deploys with such effect elsewhere: as Arthur W. Secord and, more recently, Gary Scrimgeour have shown, Defoe's scant knowledge of Africa did not extend beyond that of the average reader of contemporary travel literature.

Nonetheless, *Captain Singleton* is, if far from a sustained allegory of contemporary politics and public figures, more than a straightforward travel tale, however successful. My concern is with Defoe's polemical reasons for writing such a book, and I will argue that *Captain Singleton* can be read as a rough-and-ready contribution to contemporary political theory, as well as an exciting history of island castaways, gold-panning and piracy.

The narrative purports to be the work of the eponymous narrator, who explains how he found himself, at an early age, the cabin boy on a Portuguese galleon. After the crew mutiny, the captain puts the rebels ashore, and Singleton becomes their elected leader. The band of casta-ways sail from Madagascar to Africa, and manage to make their way across the sub-continent to the west coast. Singleton then becomes a pirate and amasses a fortune, his adventures at sea taking up approxi-mately half the text.

The earlier sections of the narrative have obvious ideological implica-tions, if we look at Defoe's recurrent use of words which carried a political charge for seventeenth- and early eighteenth-century readers. Immediately following an outburst, reminiscent of *The True-Born English-man*, against the Portuguese ("a Nation the most perfidious and the most debauch'd, the most insolent and cruel, of any that pretend to call themselves Christians, in the World"), Singleton observes that "Thiev-ing, Lying, Swearing, Forswearing, joined to the most abominable Lewd-ness, was the stated Practice of the Ship's Crew" (6). His comment evokes a long tradition of Protestant attacks on the Stuarts' supporters as crypto-Catholics addicted to profanity. As Thomas Corns points out, in parliamentary propaganda during the Civil Wars,

> Blasphemous execration, frenzied lust, and a hatred of property characterize Cavalier conduct and motivation. Swearing receives a striking prominence, and in the lists of atrocities which constitute a common feature of parliamen-tarian reportage, it assumes equal status with stripping, whipping, arbitrary executions, and mutilations.[12]

The longer discussion of swearing (not to mention whipping) in *Colonel Jack* (see below, Chapter Four) perhaps takes on new meaning in this context. One senses a whole network of signs which would have been immediately legible to contemporaries; in the early eighteenth century one's views on swearing must have been as politically revealing as one's choice of daily newspaper in the late twentieth.

Related to his characterization of the Portuguese as treacherous blas-phemers is Singleton's resentment at being the "Slave" rather than the "Servant" of his master. Work by Stephen Zwicker and Howard Erskine-Hill has sensitized us to the connotations of terms such as "slavery" in the post-Civil War period,[13] and *The True-Born Englishman*'s reference to the Norman Conquest is evidence that Defoe had employed this emotive idea elsewhere. John Locke, whose political philosophy was a pervasive influence on *Captain Singleton*, opened the first of his *Two Treatises of Government* (1690) with the following uncompromising statement:

SLAVERY is so vile and miserable an estate of man, and so directly opposite to the generous temper and courage of our nation, that it is hardly to be conceived that an "Englishman," much less a "gentleman," should plead for it.[14]

For Locke, as for the author of *The True-Born Englishman*, the repudiation of slavery is a matter of national identity as well as principle. Later in *Captain Singleton* the hero's closest companion will argue that slaves have an inherent right to rebel against their captors, having had "the highest Injustice done them" (157).

Elsewhere the language of the novel is even more overtly political in tone. When a ship's captain causes a mutiny through his imperious inflexibility, he is pleased to compare it with "Treason in the King's palace" (5-6). When the mutiny dies down, his oratory is not persuasive enough to prevent the crew falling into "Juncto's and Cabals"; "cabal," like "junto," had particularly strong associations with the anti-Stuart side from the mid-seventeenth century to the reigns of William III and Anne (see *OED*). After being expelled from the ship the mutineers form an "Assembly" (23); Singleton, who eventually becomes their leader by general consent, eventually takes the Quaker William as his "Privy-Counsellor" (168).

As these terms suggest, Defoe's concern is with core political and constitutional issues: absolutism, contractual government, and property. Having examined the language he uses to point up these themes, I shall explore each of them in more depth, though I am not suggesting that Defoe deals with them in any thoroughgoing or sophisticated way. In this I differ from Timothy Blackburn, who argues that *Captain Singleton* is an out-and-out fictionalization of Locke's political philosophy in which the protagonist progresses neatly from a state of nature to one of reason and thence to civil society. That paradigm runs into difficulties in the piracy section of the novel since, as Blackburn himself concedes, the pirates' adventures reflect a state of war, not civil order. Equally, the preceding African section of the novel, despite its setting, is not about men in a state of nature but the importance of contractual government. Politics were central to Defoe's purposes, but he was concerned with practical issues, rather than abstract theories. Indeed his impulses are sometimes more worldly than critics would like them to be, as I shall explain in my conclusion.

Like *Memoirs of a Cavalier*, *Captain Singleton* foregrounds the issue of absolutism in its portrayal of the relationship between the protagonist as a child and his father (in Singleton's case, a surrogate). In *Memoirs of a*

Cavalier the kindness and latitude extended to the Cavalier by his father is juxtaposed with the rigidly authoritarian approach to fatherhood of the Stuart kings, and hence, by implication, with their arbitrary rule. In *Captain Singleton* the hero enjoys a fleeting taste of paternal benevolence from his first (English) master, only to be captured by the Portuguese and placed under the doubtful protection of a shifty pilot on a galleon bound for the East Indies. The pilot expects Singleton to work for nothing—he wants, as Singleton puts it, to "make his Market of me" (7)—and threatens him with the Inquisition when he objects. Worse still, the ship's priest takes advantage of Singleton's lack of education to seduce him into the Catholic faith, while the pilot subjects him to a humiliating physical examination in order to discover whether he is circumcised and, therefore, a Turk. Before long he is being starved and beaten.

That there is an anti-Stuart subtext to this section of the narrative is borne out by the result of this tyranny. Singleton's desperation is such that he begins to plot his master's murder, but before he can carry out his plans the high-handedness of the captain causes the entire crew to mutiny. Responsibility for this lies fairly and squarely with the captain himself, at least in Defoe's view, as is clear from the narrator's mitigating statement that there was "some Deficiency" in the men's allowance which prompted them to rise up (10). Though the mutiny is described as an act of "Mischief" (a word which had much stronger connotations of wickedness in 1720 than it does now), the captain's reaction is immoderate: "made desperate by his Danger," he initially threatens to execute all the rebels.

Defoe's point in relating this affair is indicated firstly by his use of politically resonant terms, some of which I have already noted— "Fidelity" (15), "Treason," "Duty," "Traytors," "Cabals" (16)—and second, by the evident delight the hero takes in his emergence as the castaways' leader. Singleton does not become a despot, but the reader feels he might do so on a number of occasions, his asides being enough to illustrate the latent ambition of all those in positions of authority. His dreams of finding a ship, for example, are bound up with fantasies of limitless power:

> I used to say to them very often, that if I had but a Ship of 20 Guns, and a Sloop, and both well Manned, I would not desire a better Place in the World to make my self as rich as a King. (36)

Defoe is careful to emphasize that Singleton is voted leader by the other men, and that he is strikingly democratic, honourable and just, at least towards his companions. In this he resembles the Black Prince whom the castaways encounter after they make their way from Madagascar to Africa. In some respects the Prince is reminiscent of Aphra Behn's Oroonoko,[15] but whereas for Behn Oroonoko is the type of a royal martyr, and she incessantly stresses his nobility, dignity and suffering in order to draw an implicit comparison with Charles I,[16] for Defoe the Black Prince is simply a loved and respected leader who rules his subjects effectively and without force. He is always willing to appeal to his men's good sense, a strategy which is highly successful. He is personally brave, as well as intelligent. And he is endowed with practical skill, in this resembling the capable Gustavus Adolphus of *Memoirs of a Cavalier*. It is hard to conjure an image further removed from that of ceremonial Stuart kingship than this:

> We were now upon our Work [i.e., journey across the desert], and our Black Prince was Head Surveyor, for he was an excellent Matt-Maker himself, and all his Men understood it; so that they soon made us near a Hundred Matts. (84)

On the next page the Prince helps Singleton's men to grub up parsnips.

Singleton's own qualities of leadership become increasingly evident in the second half of the narrative, which deals with his career as a pirate. He repeatedly demonstrates his openness to advice, the respect in which his opinions are held by his co-pirates (145), and his skills of persuasion (167, 172, 184). He is shrewd and self-interested, but never tyrannical or inflexible, as though mindful of his first captain's errors of judgment in dealing with his restive crew. When his men insist on a course of action contrary to his own proposal, he recognizes the need to give in.

Other leaders in the novel are less like the Black Prince and more like the ship's captain. In the interpolated tale of Robert Knox, taken captive by the people of Ceylon, Defoe portrays a hierarchical and barbaric society. Ceylon's king is suspicious and much given to taxation, and Knox's only solace is his meagre library, which consists of two well-known Protestant texts, the Bishop of Bangor's *Practice of Piety* (1620) and Richard Rogers's *Seven Treatises Leading and Guiding to True Happiness* (1603); later he is given an English bible. The readiness of a local governor to accept bribes from the fugitive Knox, and a reference to a "Flight of the Relations of certain Nobles whom the King had clapt up" (246), makes Ceylon, for all its exotic place-names and foodstuffs, sound reminscent of Restoration England.[17] Knox's delivery is finally effected by the Dutch, ending "Nineteen Years and six months" of suffering, a period exactly equivalent to that between 1629, the beginning of Charles I's Personal Rule and the end of the Second Civil War in 1648. This may be mere coincidence, but a convincing case has been made by Manuel Schonhorn for a similarly sly parallel between Robinson Crusoe's twenty-eight year exile and the period between the Restoration and the Glorious Revolution.[18] Defoe's well-known relish for significant dates and providential "concurrences" will be further discussed in Chapter Four.

As always with Defoe, politics are inseparable from religion. Apart from Robert Knox, we also learn about thirteen Englishmen marooned on the north coast of Japan who are barely tolerated by the Japanese king and frequently approached by one of his evangelizing priests. William the Quaker argues strenuously for trying to rescue them, using terms which are sectarian as well as nationalistic:

> He told us, that . . . it was nothing but to recover Thirteen honest poor Men from a kind of Captivity, which they would otherwise never be redeemed from, and where perhaps they might some time or other be murdered by the barbarous People, in Defence of their Idolatry. (203)

Defoe raises the issue of absolutism in *Captain Singleton*, then, not only by depicting various kinds of leadership but also by associating political absolutism with religious tyranny. A natural corollary to the critique of absolutism is the exploration of alternative modes of government and, like Locke, Defoe does indeed proceed from one to the other. Ideas of the social contract and contractual monarchy are central to his novel.

As Singleton frequently points out, the mutineers formulate legislation to prevent any of their number becoming a tyrant like the captain who cast them ashore. Their innate reason is suggested by their applause for "the Captain's Generosity" (19) in furnishing them with food and ammunition, and their first act of independence is a declaration of their mutual loyalty, commitment to equality of wealth, and belief in fair representation. For seventeenth-century Whiggish political theorists such as Locke, the crucial moment in the establishment of a society is the recognition of the need for self-protection, a need which outweighs men's[19] natural desire for perfect freedom, and which leads to the making of a pact or contract.[20] Singleton and his friends mark their transition from a "primitive" state of nature to a commonwealth in terms which echo Locke's second *Treatise*:

> the first thing we did was to give every one his hand, that we would not separate from one another upon any Occasion whatsoever, but that we would

live and die together; that we would kill no Food, but that we would distribute it in publick; and that we would be in all things guided by the Majority.   (20)

In distinguishing between temporary contracts, such as those made in trading, and compacts which transform a group of men into a society, Locke had stressed the same principles of mutuality, cohesion and self-defence:

Political power, then, I take to be a right of making laws, with penalties of death, and consequently all less penalties for the regulating and preserving of property, and of employing the force of the community in the execution of such laws, and in the defence of the commonwealth from foreign injury, and all this only for the public good.   (118)

The extent of Defoe's knowledge of Locke is unclear, but that there is some influence, albeit at one or more remove, is unquestionable. As Geoffrey Holmes has pointed out, William III's Declaration justifying his invasion of 1688 uses a vocabulary "near-interchangeable" with that of the second *Treatise*, and Defoe must have known the Declaration, for as early as 1689 he had contributed to the long pamphlet war with the Jacobites following William's accession.[21] Moreover, as Holmes also insists, citing the work of Richard Ashcraft,[22] there was a marked continuity between the work of major commentators on the constitution such as Locke, Sidney, James Tyrrell and Henry Neville, and the "humbler level of hundreds of lesser tracts and pamphlets published in the Exclusionist cause from 1679 to 1681" (160, 138).

Extrapolating from this evidence of top-down influence in an earlier period, it seems only reasonable to assume that Defoe was familiar with Locke's ideas, if not his actual text, though in fact he could certainly afford to have purchased the *Two Treatises* in book form, and may well have done so.[23] His most recent biographer argues that, like his teacher Andrew Morton, Defoe "adhered to the theory of contract government, and . . . consistently defended it all his life. [He] relied primarily on biblical precedent and what we now consider Lockean arguments for the moral right of revolution" (Backscheider 49).

The commonwealth established by the castaways in *Captain Singleton* is undoubtedly closer to a contractual monarchy than a democracy, as we might expect given Defoe's devotion to William III. Although the men are to choose a leader on a rotating basis, there are no elections as such, and the men are as obligated to obey him as he is to consult them. As though to highlight the civility inherent in these "Rules," Singleton describes the neighbouring natives as "an ignorant, ravenous, brutish sort of People," and as "scarce human, or capable of being made sociable on any Account whatsoever" (21). By contrast with these natives, whose co-operation with one another and the castaways is seen as cunning rather than civilized, Singleton's men act only for the general good, and habitually discuss alternative courses of action before reaching peaceful agreements. Such discussions are referred to as the "Counsels of this Assembly" (23) by Singleton, who represents himself as having special authority. His method is always to distance himself from the early stages of discussion, the better to intervene with considered advice. In persuading the men to adopt his escape plan—which is to build a small sea canoe in order to capture an ocean-going ship—his judicious contribution to the "General Consultations" (24) finds instant favour, and any ethical objections to it are swept away in the excitement.

Yet Singleton, like the Cavalier, is not to be taken wholly at his own estimation. His confident account of his successes as leader is undermined by occasional admissions that contractual government has not produced a society without crime. From the opening of the novel we have been encouraged to regard him critically and sceptically; he began with an ironic gesture of deference to the conventions of autobiography ("I can look but a very little Way into my Pedigree" [1]), and in chronicling the castaways' consensual approach to problem-solving he is as much concerned to boast about his own leadership style as to illustrate the amicability of their discussions. He is frankly amused at his own plausibility when he appears to assent to the principle of common ownership:

> The two Peices of Eight I shewed, and one Moydore, but no more; and none of them ever suspected that I had any more Money in the World, having been known to be only a poor Boy taken up in Charity, as you have heard, and used like a Slave. (20)

The artfully plaintive accents are exactly like those of Colonel Jack during his interrogation by the Quaker's clerk.[24]

It is not immediately obvious what Defoe means by Singleton's covert disregard for the rules he otherwise represents as the only means to a just and safe society. His money never proves useful to him, and he later holds faithful to the agreement that all the panned gold the company find in Africa will be added to the "common Stock" (128). It is divided with impeccable fairness after the trek across the sub-continent. For Defoe, however, as for Hobbes and even Locke, the body politic is a consequence of men's need to protect themselves from one another, and Singleton's avaricious self-interest bears out rather than controverts this need.

Like many of Defoe's protagonists, Singleton is an energetic and intelligent rogue who gradually succumbs to the temptations of crime. The second half of his narrative, which describes his bloodthirsty exploits as a pirate, is only superficially closer to Hobbes than the first half; while the two sections may not be intended to have the complementary functions of Parts I and II of *Memoirs of a Cavalier* (they are not formally divided), there is no glaring inconsistency between their respective views of human nature and political society. Both illustrate the necessity for a society based on contractual government and the ease with which criminals can subvert the state. Locke had sought, after all, to demonstrate the benefits of contractual government, not to argue for its inevitability. Indeed the reverse: in the *Two Treatises* he feels obliged repeatedly to attack absolutism. To Defoe, too, historical evidence suggested that early societies were highly illiberal. As he explains in *A General History of Discoveries and Useful Arts* (1725-26),

> they [i.e. people in biblical times] seem'd for some Ages under the mere Law of Nature; their Government was Patriarchal, the Father of every Tribe being the Sovereign, or King of all the subsequent Branches; every other Father, having Families of their own begetting, bare Rule, as so many Viceroys under the Patriarchal Monarch, as long as he liv'd; and thus they went on, till several Tribes encreasing, and growing Populous, made themselves Kings and Governors; who, as it continued for many Years after, Governed whole Cities, with the Districts belonging to them, as absolute Monarch, and whom no Man durst disobey, on the Penalty of Life. (14)

According to Defoe, men may behave with the utmost civility and gentleness: Avery's treatment of his prisoners in *The King of Pirates*, for instance, is exemplary.[25] But they are equally capable of shocking cruelty. In the second half of *Captain Singleton* the hero and his friends immolate and then mortar-bomb a group of New Guineans in a giant hollow tree, and as pirates they are as predatory and reckless as the most brutish natives they encounter.

What is more, the bonds of fellowship between the pirates are weaker than those which united the castaways. Singleton remains unusually blessed with the power to influence his men, but they are altogether more desperate than his first companions. When they discover that a ship of Negro captives has murdered its white crew, they can scarcely be restrained from murdering the lot. William's arguments, however, win the day, and are important for the light they shed on Defoe's political philosophy:

the Negroes had really the highest Injustice done them, to be sold for Slaves without their Consent; and that the Law of Nature dictated to them; that they ought not to kill them, and that it would be wilful Murder to do it. (157)

The Law of Nature is used here in its Lockean sense of the right to self-protection.

As we see, for Defoe as for Locke, the social contract is not antithetical to nature but founded on natural principles of justice. The tendency of men to violence is precisely what necessitates the body politic; the castaways defined "Law[s]" (50) and practiced "State" (35) in order to "defend [them]selves" (20), and the pirates, Negro captives and even the Portuguese are merely manifesting man's innate tendencies towards competition. Men can choose contractual government—and peace and prosperity—or they can choose to live in a "state of Nature" which is the opposite of lawful.

If *Captain Singleton*'s emphasis on the savagery of pirates is not just for dramatic effect (such stories were very popular with readers), neither is it designed merely to illustrate an abstract point about human nature. Much has been written about Defoe's interest in piracy[26]—and some questions asked about the actual extent of his writings on the subject[27]— but it should be borne in mind that, as well as illustrating his keen sense of the large commercial readership for criminal biographies, his pirate narratives express the very real anxieties of the legitimate trader. By stressing, as critics have often done, the eclecticism of Defoe's career, both literary and non-literary, it is easy to forget that he owned very substantial property and belonged, for all his many business failures, to the prosperous mercantile society of post-Restoration London. He had been, for example, Butler of the Cornhill Inquest, and was elected to the Cornhill Grand Jury in 1690,[28] as well as owning business interests worth many thousands of pounds.[29] In 1707 he had written an issue of the *Review* on the topic of the Madagascar pirates, and after one satirical thrust at the expense of certain piratical merchants on the London Exchange he offered a serious analysis of high-seas piracy which stressed the danger it posed to honest traders. In August 1688 Defoe had sold his share in a ship to a merchant, Robert Harrison, who shortly afterwards took the ship to Portugal only to be captured by a man-of-war. Defoe was sued in Chancery for his share in the loss; the details of the case are obscure,[30] but it must have contributed to his preoccupation with the scourge of piracy in his later years. The tone of the *Review* is almost shrill in urging action on the government, that such a Nest of Desperadoes may be rooted out, before they grow too strong, and the Disease incurable; before it grow a common Practice to run away with Ships, rob, plunder and destroy, and run thither for Shelter. If all the Banditti, the Murtherers and Vagabonds of *Europe*, should once fix this Place in their Eye, who knows how strong it may grow. (427)

Yet many buccaneers would, Mr Review insists, lead a reformed life if they were allowed to return home without fear of penalty, a view which is endorsed in *Captain Singleton* and which represents a pragmatic view of crime rather than a morally lax one. In 1707 Defoe saw no other solution to the worsening situation than an amnesty, pirates being so well-established along the world's major trading routes that it would be impossible to eradicate them by force.

His view was evidently unchanged by 1720, for he has Avery, a historical pirate who makes a fictional appearance in *Captain Singleton*, suggest to the hero that they consolidate their achievements by building "a little City" in Madagascar, and Singleton is of much the same mind, though he would prefer a more pastoral way of life in future:

> thus Planting the high Ground with Cattle, such as Cows and Goats, of which the Country also was full, to be sure we might live here as well as any Men in the World; and I owned to him, I thought it was a good Retreat for those that were willing to leave off, and lay down, and yet did not care to venture home and be hanged. (182)

The inference is unmistakable: whilst pirates remain in inaccessible regions their stranglehold on trade will be resisted only at great cost, and they will renounce their criminal activities only if they are pardoned by their native countries. The *Review* makes the additional point that punishing pirates such as Avery with fines would be a source of revenue for the government.

Piracy in *Captain Singleton*, then, is a real socio-economic problem with tangible consequences. The novel is an extended argument in favour of international legislation on global shipping, showing that the current lawlessness of the seas is responsible for the kidnapping trade, the brutal practices of the slave triangle, and generally for unimaginable losses of life and property. The timing of the book's publication is probably significant: one historian suggests that "Perhaps the peak of pirate barbarity came around 1720."[31]

Political theory is central to the novel's treatment of piracy, however, since Defoe's ultimate aim is to prove the need for strong and effective government at home and abroad. He does so by revealing the aggression on which the social contract is founded and the security it provides from the violence of others. A successful government would not be tyrannical or brutal—as are those of Portugal and Spain, for example—but would be committed to safeguarding the economic interests of England and its merchants. The point is deeply party political, for the resentment caused by the Stuarts' indifference to the mercantile interest can be traced back to the 1620s, and Chapter 5 of Locke's second *Treatise* is pointedly entitled "Of Property." Charles II and James II were thought to have abandoned English shipping to privateers, and one cause of Defoe's intense loyalty to William III had been William's success in protecting England's trading routes (Holmes, *Great Power* 160). *Captain Singleton* is an affirmation that piracy remains a critical problem for the nation's economy in 1720, and it demonstrates the urgent need for a government which will tackle crime. As so often with Defoe, the text is "soft" on social issues and "hard" on law and order, confirming that he is perhaps best understood as a progressive rather than a radical. Like Locke's, his attitudes to property were inherently contradictory, as further investigation reveals.

In the *Two Treatises* Locke had defended common ownership, suggesting that it had been a feature of the earliest societies. In a world of seemingly limitless natural resources men's property rights had arisen from the labour they expended in helping themselves to the common stock. Yet despite his description of this primitivist utopia, Locke's belief in equal wealth was far from absolute: he also suggested that some people deserve more than others, on the grounds that some are more "industrious and rational" than others (132). Indeed, civil society has rightly instituted compacts or laws to protect the rights of those who have accumulated more than they need. At moments, however, Locke betrays a certain uneasiness with his argument as, for example, when he blames money for producing social conflict:

> this I dare boldly affirm, that the same rule of propriety—viz., that every man should have as much as he could make use of—would hold still in the world, without straitening anybody . . . had not the invention of money . . . introduced larger possessions. (134)

Perhaps sensing the radicalism implicit in this aside, he neglects to pursue the problems caused by unequal property rights any further.

Partly as a consequence of Locke's decision to gloss over these problems, subsequent writers were able to use the *Two Treatises* to defend the ascendancy of the Whig merchant classes without acknowledging that their cherished rights of individual freedom and property were protected at the unacknowledged expense of others. As one historian puts it, after Locke the idea of the State of Nature "came to be used as a means whereby the new ruling classes could vindicate, against the surviving restraints of the old feudal and ecclesiastical order, their cherished rights of individual freedom and of property."[32] Not until Marx would anyone follow through to its logical conclusion Locke's suggestion that "Of the products of the earth useful to the life of man, nine-tenths are the effects of labour" (136).

Far more so than Locke, Defoe has been brought to book by modern commentators for the ethical inconsistencies of his liberalism. He has been repeatedly condemned for the acquisitiveness of his protagonists and for the insincerity of their pious outbursts against material greed, a number of critics being sceptical of the idea that he intended to place an ironic distance between himself and his roguish protagonists. While I will discuss the limitations of this scepticism in my chapter on *Moll Flanders*, there is a modicum of truth in the argument that a novel such as *Captain Singleton* deplores its hero's greed on the one hand while celebrating his financial successes on the other.

It could be argued, however, that Defoe was simply less squeamish than Locke about the self-interest at the heart of the Whig position on property rights. Few Whigs saw a conflict between their opposition to Stuart absolutism, and their support for imperialist expansion and industrial capitalism, even though they were exchanging one tyranny for another, their own. Defoe, for example, disapproves of the bully who enslaves Singleton as a cabin boy, but later hesitates to condemn Singleton himself for his naked avarice. Nor does he object to the white men's automatic subjugation of the natives they encounter, and numerous incidents in the novel illustrate his belief that the acquisition of property is the strongest human instinct. His willingness to suggest openly that some people are entitled to be richer than others may be unpalatable, but it would be wrong to blame him for a contradiction fundamental to post-Revolutionary political philosophy in general.

The whole question of property rights was an incendiary one in a period which had seen a monarch brought down over taxation, wardships and royal monopolies. Locke and later Whigs were concerned to defend property not out of any proto-communist sense of social justice but because property had been, and remained, at the heart of parliamentary objections to the Stuarts. During the Civil War, Puritan propaganda had persistently characterized the Cavaliers as the extravagant despoilers of other men's property, and Restoration royalists had flaunted their decadent habits in the face of Puritans thought hostile to indulgence and luxury. According to Locke and other Whig writers such as Shaftesbury, Charles II and James II were to be resisted for, among other things, the threat they posed to property, and trade in particular. Likewise, for a merchant such as Defoe, whose livelihood had derived from London's commercial expansion as an entrepôt port, property, in terms of the safety of English shipping, was an urgent political issue. As I have said, William's popularity with the Whigs had been inextricably bound up with his determination to defend the country's mercantile interest against Catholic aggressors, the slogan "popery and wooden shoes" appropriately conflating religious and economic oppression.

The political philosophy embodied in *Captain Singleton* is, then, all of a piece, for the question of property has brought us back to the question of absolutism versus contractual monarchy. The first half of *Captain Singleton* describes the fortunes of a group of men who resist a tyrant and institute a kind of commonwealth, one in which the monarch is chosen by common consent on grounds of personal merit. This monarch, or captain, is bound to consult his men before taking decisions; equally, they are bound to obey him. Property is held in common, and that Singleton confesses to keeping back a few moidores for himself is in fact proof of the need for strong social bonds rather than an indication that the little commonwealth is flawed from within. When the castaways finally reach a suitable port they are still holding true to their principles of mutuality and commonality, and have amassed a fortune into the bargain.

In the second half of the narrative we see the consequences to property of a government which fails to enforce the law on the high seas. Virtually unchecked, save by each other, the pirate kings of the southern hemisphere seize and stockpile treasures, and jeopardize vital trading routes such as the Red Sea and key ports such as Hormuz. As with petty crime among the street children in *Colonel Jack*, some of their piracies may be due to necessity: thrown onto their own resources at the beginning of the novel, Singleton and his men resolve to provide for themselves "by fair Means or foul" (78), and doubtless some actual pirates were forced to do the same. But as a fully-fledged pirate Singleton is completely without conscience, stealing far more than he could ever need. His criminal disposition is emphasized by his ironic appreciation of William's Quakerish cunning in refusing to admit his willingness to "go on the account" (144), i.e., formally join the pirate community.[33] Should the ship be taken, William can always plead that he was abducted.

William's disarmingly disingenuous personality typifies Defoe's contradictory attitude to criminals in his novels. On the one hand he regards the pirates as a scourge, and on the other he cannot help acknowledging their attractiveness. As Singleton says, "I think the giving an Account of some of my other Adventures may be an agreeable Piece of Story" (139), and it is. The second half of the book amounts to a rapid, highly circumstantial description of his piratical career in which there is often little room for reflection, moral or otherwise.

At the very end Singleton is converted to an honest life, but even then he is motivated less by a genuine sense that he has acquired enough wealth, than by William's desire to go home. Yet Singleton himself feels he has no home, and clearly, as with Colonel Jack, his childhood experiences are partly responsible for his amorality as an adult: "I was a kind of Charity School-Boy, so that I can have no Desire of going any where for being rich or poor, for I have no where to go" (256). The account of his brutalization as a cabin boy, underlined by this recollection, anticipates the urgent demands in *Colonel Jack* for the widespread setting up of charity schools to deal with the nation's orphans. Ultimately *Captain Singleton* sees piracy as an urgent economic problem arising directly from social neglect and inadequate state protection for shipping. The real-life Captain Avery who appears in *Captain Singleton* lived very much as his fictional counterpart relates, in a colony with complete immunity to the law:

> Captain Avery, to give him his due, proposed our building a little City here, establishing our selves on Shore, with a good Fortification, and Works proper to defend our selves; and that, as we had Wealth enough, and could encrease it to what Degree we pleased, we should content our selves to retire here, and bid Defiance to the World. (182)

As Mr Review had truculently pointed out to those advocating the eradication of piracy by force,

> you cannot do it . . . but you must plant a Colony there, possess the Island, which is bigger than our three Kingdoms, that were; then you must maintain Men of War always there, to cruise and awe them, or if not, wherever you drive them, they will return. (427)

The only solution was to allow pirates to return on the understanding that they pay a financial price, and in *Captain Singleton* Defoe defended this very policy. In response to the escalation in piracy after 1713 (when the Treaty of Utrecht had put an end to the rampant but lawful privateering in the waters around Virginia) a royal proclamation had been issued promising pardons to all piracies committed before

66

5 January 1718, so long as the offenders turned themselves in. As Rankin explains:

> This was a remarkable document in that the pirates were forgiven all murders they had committed, and they were allowed to retain their accumulated loot. In a sense, it was an open admission that the situation had grown desperate and was out of the control of government. (90-91)

Captain Singleton might seem to typify Defoe's inability to resist a successful individualist, however questionable his morals; critics have sometimes suggested that *Moll Flanders* is similarly compromised by its refusal to mete out punishment to its seasoned criminal of a heroine. Perhaps Defoe does share a little of our own delicious horror at Singleton's frank admissions of his crimes, or Moll's casual attitude to hers, but his main concern, as with his other protagonists, is the alarming ease with which they operate. Honest merchant-venturers are a soft target for Singleton, just as simple shop-keepers are no match for Moll. The more outrageous their actions, the more fearful we are meant to feel about the proliferation of crime, even if we cannot help also feeling some amusement at their bare-faced cheek. The question, then, is not whether Defoe is ironic in his portrayals of Singleton, Moll and Jack, but why. Such characters are intended, I believe, to force the reader's wry acknowledgment of an urgent social and economic problem. They stem from exactly the same anxieties as those which produced the notorious Black Act of 1723, and which led to a dramatic increase in the number of capital offences on the statute books in the late seventeenth and early eighteenth centuries. Singleton's audacity may be thrilling, but it must have spoken to the genuine fears of anyone with a vested interest in international trade.

As I have acknowledged, *Captain Singleton* is not a comprehensive working-out of Locke's theories of government: its engagement with political theory is simplistic and at times cursory. It is, however, a logical and effective illustration both of the dangers of arbitrary government, and of the needs for contractual monarchy and adequate state protection of private property. Its philosophy boils down to this: despotism produces rebellion, while government by mutual consent leads to peace and prosperity. As Singleton's adventures as a pirate demonstrate, a state indifferent to the property of its law-abiding—and wealth-creating—citizens allows lawlessness and violence to flourish unchecked. The scale of the problem is brought home to the reader by the geographical breadth of *Captain Singleton*: ruthless crews infest the seas from the West Indies to Indo-China.

Because of the strong association between Whig supporters of William III and the commercial and mercantile classes of post-Restoration England, *Captain Singleton*'s exciting account of castaways and buccaneers carries a political charge which time may have obscured. If we are fully to appreciate Defoe's aims, we need to refresh our memories regarding the special connotations of terms such as "Assembly" and "Cabals," regarding issues such as parental tyranny, and regarding ideas such as the "Law of Nature." If we try to read *Captain Singleton* as a primitive first-person novel which foreshadows the mature fictional biographies of later novelists such as Fielding, Sterne and Austen, it will seem lacking in psychological insight and narrative structure. But if instead we read it as a resourceful, improvisatory response to contemporary ideological conflicts, we understand precisely why its protagonist can, on the one hand, offer a scathing critique of absolutism and, on the other, cheerfully admit to a series of brutal crimes against persons and property. From Defoe's point of view Singleton the rebel and Singleton the outlaw are mutually compatible exemplifications of the pressing need for just, lawful, and responsible government.

CHAPTER THREE

Moll Flanders: Urban Guerrilla

One late twentieth-century school of thought on crime prevention favours the fitting of security devices on cars, the setting up of neighbourhood-watch schemes, and the wiring of private houses with burglar alarms. In other words, one should erect physical barriers between the criminal and the source of his or her temptation, property. While advocates of this approach do not always deny the significance of environmental factors in the creation of criminal offenders, they regard them as of secondary importance. On the evidence of *Moll Flanders*, Defoe would have found much that was sympathetic in this pragmatic if not entirely rational view, for the novel insistently warns of the threat posed by crime to the propertied classes. The more egregious the heroine's misdeeds, the more the reader is supposed to shudder at the thought of all those designing whores out there, all those reckless pickpockets, all those bare-faced robbers and cheats. Critics have frequently worried about the implications of the fact that Moll gets away with so much, wondering if Defoe was, in fact, her covert admirer. But the point he wanted to make was that real-life criminals often did get away with it, and that divine retribution could not be depended upon, being less reliable in the prevention and detection of crime than strong locks, sharp eyes, and a suspicious streak.

The preceding discussions have interpreted two of Defoe's more neglected narratives in the light of what can be known about their social, political and economic contexts. A contextual reading of *Memoirs of a Cavalier*, for example, has shown it to be an elaborate, sustained attempt to impersonate a royalist, warts and all. Similarly, a contextualized *Captain Singleton* becomes an exposé of tyranny and an exploration of alternatives to monarchical absolutism. Each of these readings presupposes a heavy irony in Defoe's view of his protagonists, and in this chapter I shall attempt to show that *Moll Flanders*, too, is a response to specific socio-political problems which uses irony to deal with them.

Since the 1950s critics have debated the relationship between Moll Flanders and her creator, some suggesting that Defoe, a shrewd businessman, took more than a modicum of delight in his heroine's material successes,[1] others feeling that there is an unmissable ironic distance between the author and his roguish, unself-conscious creation.[2] My own belief is that there is irony in *Moll Flanders*, but that it is not intended to expose Moll's confusion of earthly with spiritual rewards; rather, as I have said, it is supposed to confirm the reader's worst fears about the wicked society in which he or she lives. The more blatant Moll's actions, the more horrified our response to her. Every time she blithely confesses to a crime, and brushes any feelings of compunction aside, the respectable reader is supposed to flinch and, as a consequence, become more alert to crime. *Moll Flanders* is neither a super-subtle critique of the capitalist ethic underpinning Protestantism, nor a shameless defence of accumulation. It is, however, on the side of the economic individualist in that it urges us as property owners, rich and less rich alike, to be eternally vigilant in the war against crime, and to give credence to the terrible things we read in the papers. Its irony is not sophisticated, but crudely effective: here is a self-confessed whore and thief who, we can assume, represents the tip of a sociological iceberg.

That Moll is ubiquitous and unscrupulous is not, therefore, a cause of celebration for Defoe, but a source of extreme apprehension. To be sure, we are entertained along the way by her account, as film-goers are entertained by stories of serial killers and international terrorists. But the overwhelming impression Moll gives us is that society is held hostage by a criminal underclass which is heedless of risk and danger, and has no respect for the rights of others. Moll is the Georgian equivalent of the "urban guerrilla" who terrorises twentieth-century cities, and her story can be seen as a kind of forerunner to television shows such as *America's Most Wanted* and *Crimewatch UK.* These, too, thrillingly and terrifyingly reconstruct recent crimes in order simultaneously to solve them, derive entertainment from them, and prevent their recurrence. The crime prevention message of *Moll Flanders* runs through the whole of the novel, but I will begin with a single illustrative episode, Moll's relationship with the baronet she first encounters at Bartholomew Fair.

Bartholomew Fair had been synonymous with petty crime and disorder since at least 1614, when Ben Jonson had depicted the cutpurses, roaring boys, bawds and punks who battened on the crowds gathered at Smithfield on St. Bartholomew's Day (August 24). Moll tells the reader (untruthfully) that she had not been to Smithfield before, and regretfully admits that the "common" part of the fair (i.e., its entertainments) were not "of much advantage" to her, but she goes to it in search of easy prey. She turns into a "raffling-" or lottery-shop,[3] and meets a well-dressed gentleman who initiates a conversation with her. She is anxious the reader should understand that the gentleman engineered his own downfall, her initial role being passive:

> He held me in talk so long, till at last he drew me out of the raffling place to the shop-door, and then to a walk in the cloister, still talking of a thousand things cursorily without anything to the purpose. At last he told me that, without compliment, he was charmed with my company, and asked me if I durst trust myself in a coach with him; he told me he was a man of honour, and would not offer anything to me unbecoming him as such. I seemed to decline it a while, but suffered myself to be importuned a little, and then yielded. (217)

The critic who thinks Moll is a hypocrite and that Defoe's main concern is to satirize her will find ammunition in this apparently blatant denial of responsibility, for she is clearly searching for excuses. The critic who believes that Defoe identified strongly with Moll may, however, have some difficulties, since the idea that he is indulging her sits ill with the disapproval which the narrative directs at the kind of wealthy gentleman who would pick up a prostitute at Bartholomew Fair: "These are the men of whom Solomon says, 'They go like an ox to the slaughter, till a dart strikes through their liver'" (218). Much of the irony we detect here is directed at the gentleman himself, and its source is Moll, who has the professional whore's contempt for her sordid client. She is much more worldly-wise than he is:

> I was at a loss in my thoughts to conclude at first what this gentleman designed; but I found afterwards he had had some drink in his head, and that he was not very unwilling to have some more. He carried me in the coach to the Spring Garden, at Knightsbridge, where we walked in the gardens, and he treated me very handsomely; but I found he drank very freely. He pressed me also to drink, but I declined it. (217)

And in case any reader makes the classic error, as this gentleman does, and assumes that Moll is interested in sexual gratification, she observes that "As for the bed, etc., I was not much concerned about that part" (217). She is after only one thing: money.

The baronet pays a heavy price for his moment of pleasure, since Moll helps herself to his gold watch, his purse, his periwig, his expensive gloves, his sword and his snuff-box, an inventory which bespeaks his wealth and status. Later she refers to him as his "worship," which implies that he is either a mayor or a magistrate. (The former seems more likely, given Defoe's connections with the City of London and the systems of local government within it: *The True-Born Englishman*, for example, had pilloried at least one corrupt mayor, Edward Backwell.) Some of the

71

highest in the land are involved in the London underworld, Defoe is suggesting, and if we argue that his satire is simply at Moll's expense we would be guilty of lashing the whore while sparing the hypocritical beadle. Through Moll, who has been perfectly frank about her own motives all along, Defoe tries to shock the reader into recognising his[4] own predilections and vulnerability: "There is nothing so absurd, so surfeiting, so ridiculous, as a man heated by wine in his head, and a wicked gust in his inclination together" (218). Some newspaper reports attempt to serve a similar function today, describing how an old person in the vicinity has been robbed by a confidence-trickster posing as a life assurance salesman, or noting that the children who burned the house down had been left on their own by their parents.

Defoe uses circumstantial detail in the Bartholomew episode in order to bring his moral home to the reader. The same technique has been identified in *The Family Instructor* by Paula Backscheider, who regards it as evidence of Defoe's innovative realism. *The Family Instructor*, she notes, defends its digressions with the argument that "Circumlocutions" are necessary "to preserve the cadence of things, and introduce the substance of the real story by necessary gradations."[5] Backscheider is right to claim that "An awareness of the relationship between temporal and fictional time and of the pleasures of a good story artfully told . . . sets Defoe dramatically apart" from many of his contemporaries,[6] but Defoe's motives for pursuing realism were at least as much didactic and pragmatic as artistic. When Moll describes how she robbed her gentleman, or how her friend used to gull clients into thinking their fobpockets had not been rifled, Defoe hopes the reader will reflect on the security of his or her own gold watch.

The reason critics have been overly distracted by the problem of his likeable but appalling heroine is not hard to identify. Some twentieth-century readers continue to evince the discomfort and prurience which characterised the Victorians' reaction to *Moll Flanders*, interpreting it as a text which is primarily about a shameless, deceitful whore. Of course Defoe does subscribe to some stereotypical views of women's sexual depravity: *Roxana* as well as *Moll Flanders* is evidence of that. But his interest is also in the wider social and economic effects of crime, and he is consequently just as critical of Moll's credulous clients and naive victims as he is of her;[7] in fact he thinks she has some excuses for what she does, whereas the likes of the baronet do not.

Before analysing other ways in which *Moll Flanders* tries to raise contemporaries' consciousness of crime, we should consider both its historical context and the antecedent tradition of rogue- and whore-biographies. It would be labouring the point unduly to reiterate here the arguments about Defoe's ideological and political aims which I have expounded in previous chapters. And in any case I am not proposing that *Moll Flanders* is an anti-Jacobite or anti-Stuart novel, or a staunchly Whig-Protestant one. It does, however, like the other novels discussed, depend on our full understanding of a range of references to contemporary social and political issues. In other words, it uses the same kind of strategies they do: sly parallels, loaded allusions, "chance" similarities, topical references. When we reflect on the year in which it was published, 1722, we can scarcely avoid the likelihood that Defoe had a specific aim when he wrote it, namely to warn his readers about the consequences of a (perceived) rise in crime, especially in London.

The early 1720s have recently come to be understood as years of social, economic and political instability in England, most obviously because of the South Sea Bubble but for other reasons too. E. P. Thompson has suggested that it may be justifiable to talk of a "crime wave" in the early 1720s:

> a combination of factors (the profound corruption of the enforcement authorities, the "blood-money" system of rewards, the bankruptcies and poverty in the wake of the Bubble, an acute crisis of genuine gang warfare between [Jonathan] Wild and his competitors) had led to a high incidence of crimes of robbery and violence and to a heightened awareness of the dangers from footpads and highwaymen.[8]

As I have tried to demonstrate, Defoe's novels, like his other writings, were almost always written in response to their historical circumstances. In 1718, for example, the year of the Earl of Mar's uprising, he wrote the strongly anti-Jacobite *Memoirs of Majr. Alexander Ramkins, A Highland Officer*;[9] while in 1722, the year of the Atterbury plot, he published *Colonel Jack*. In the same year, which Thompson depicts as one of widespread and excessive anxiety about crime, Defoe produced *Moll Flanders*, in which, as in *Colonel Jack*, he deals extensively with the issues of crime, transportation and rehabilitation. In 1724 these novels were followed by an account of the life of the thief Jack Sheppard and, in 1725, a life of Jonathan Wild.[10] More was to come: John Robert Moore attributes to Defoe *A Brief Historical Account of the Lives of the Six Notorious Street-Robbers* (1726), *Some Considerations Upon Street-Walkers* (1726), and brief sketches such as *Street Robberies, Consider'd* (1728).[11]

Not surprisingly, then, though *Moll Flanders* purports to have been written in 1683, its concern is with the present; and its London is recognisable as the prosperous, sprawling capital of the 1720s, with the suburbs so enthusiastically described in *A Tour Through the Whole Island of Great Britain* (1724-26).[12] At the same time the text reminds us that Defoe's perspective was that of someone who had grown up in the Restoration. We have always to remember that he was forty by the turn of the century, and that in 1722 he was in his sixties; too much stress on his citizenry of the modern world can lead us to forget that the whole of his youth was passed under Stuart rule. The young woman in *Religious Courtship* who was so sure no Jacobite gentleman would ever impose on her was reminded by her elder sister of a lesson in recent history:

> I have heard, that in King Charles the Second's time, people in general were deluded with that very expression in all their public speeches, proclamations, declarations, &c., promising always to preserve and maintain the church of England, as established by law; and yet all that while they meant the popish church.[13]

This readiness to draw parallels with recent history is quintessentially Defovean, and reflects a widespread fear among contemporaries that the turmoil of the Civil War and its aftermath would once more disrupt national life. As in many of Defoe's works, his great anxiety in *Moll Flanders* is that the troubles of the previous century will recur in the present, or that they have already done so. Like *Colonel Jack, Moll Flanders* evokes the disorder of late seventeenth-century London quite as much as it does the more expansive one of 1722, but does so in order to comment on the problems of renewed urban crime and disorder. In the 1720s society was felt to be succumbing to crime at every level, not just amongst the poor. As Thompson says, "It was in these years that the comparison of statesmanship with criminality became common coinage" in literature (*Whigs and Hunters* 216-17).

It would, of course, be wrong to identify the 1720s with a single, homogeneous view of crime. As we might expect, given his equivocal attitude to George I and Robert Walpole, Defoe's progressive attitude to criminal offenders (he recommended transportation rather than hanging, and was opposed to corporal punishment) is much more reminiscent of the late seventeenth century than the brutal and punitive 1720s. He was also revolutionary in his emphasis on property crime rather than crimes against the person. Douglas Hay, who has written extensively on crime in the early modern period, is scathing about the ruling-class ideology of the Glorious Revolution, but his remarks are suggestive for an understanding of Defoe:

> The Glorious Revolution of 1688 established the freedom not of men, but of men of property. Its apologist, John Locke, distorted the oldest arguments of

natural law to justify the liberation of wealth from all political or moral controls; he concluded that the unfettered accumulation of money, goods and land was sanctioned by Nature and, implicitly, by God.[14]

We have already seen the extent to which *Captain Singleton* affirmed Lockean rights of property, and though commentators have been at pains to point out that property for Locke included the individual's own body, Defoe is as inclined as Locke to talk about property in terms of land, crops and mineral resources. He was a man of substance himself, and left plenty of legal evidence to suggest that he defended his property with determination. For Alan Macfarlane early modern crime typically involved money and private property rather than violence— "Theft, a characteristically 'bourgeois' or capitalist crime, has been the central and most persecuted offence in England since at least the fourteenth century"[15]—and it is noticeable that the crimes he lists all feature in *Moll Flanders*: tampering with the coinage, theft, burglaries, highway robberies. Defoe hardly considers violent crime, except where violence might be used to conceal a crime of property.

Moll Flanders should also be understood in the context of the intensification of the penal code in the last decades of the seventeenth century and the first two of the eighteenth. Hay ("Property" 18) cites Leon Radzinowicz, who estimates that the number of capital statutes rose from around 50 to 200 between 1688 and 1720, and we might expect literature on crime to have flourished in this period. The *Newgate Calendar* began in 1700, and by the 1720s, according to Backscheider, the craze for crime-stories was at its height:

> The broadsides ballads, chapbooks, newspapers, pamphlets, "anatomies," and criminal characters of the sixteenth and seventeenth centuries were augmented by the *Old Bailey Sessions Papers, The Ordinary of Newgate, his Account,* and collections such as *A Compleat Collection of Remarkable Tryals* and *The History of the Lives of the Most Noted Highway-men*. From the beginning, pirates were included with domestic housebreakers, infanticides, and frustrated lovers, and travel was often a part of the larger crime stories.[16]

These works, like *Moll Flanders*, both reflected and contributed to public concerns about crime and the moral condition of the nation. One eighteenth-century historian looking back at the 1720s noted that Walpole had suspended the Habeas Corpus Act in 1722, and had only this to say of the years 1718 to 1726:

> This was the age of interested projects, inspired by a venal spirit of adventure, the natural consequence of that avarice, fraud, and profligacy, which the monied corporations had introduced. This of all others is the most unfavour-

able æra for an historian. A reader of sentiment and imagination cannot be entertained or interested by a dry detail of such transactions as admit of no warmth, no colouring, no embellishment, a detail which serves only to exhibit an inanimate picture of tasteless vice and mean degeneracy.[17]

Traditional studies of early eighteenth-century crime literature have tended to overlook its historical context, concentrating instead on its literary qualities and its role in the rise of the novel. In particular, rogue and whore biographies have been implicitly admired for promoting a kind of realism which anticipated that of novelists such as Richardson and Smollett. Though some critics, such as John Richetti, have tried to acknowledge the ideological function of criminal literature, they have emphasized its escapist appeal, and downplayed the extent to which rogue biographies scapegoated criminals or encouraged their readers' fears of robbers and con-artists. Richetti regards the insistence in rogue histories on the unregenerate nature of the hero or heroine as "conventional moralizing," put in to offset the titillation, escapism and vicarious triumphs over the law offered in these texts.[18]

I would argue that although it may be true some narratives sought to keep their readers to the straight and narrow, or, by contrast, invited them to identify with daring criminals, most aimed to strike terror into their readers' hearts. One story in the *History of the Lives and Robberies of the Most Noted Highway-men* (1713), cited by Richetti, shows exactly what contemporaries feared would happen to honest citizens if they came up against a ruthless criminal:

> The Maid then upbraiding him [a fellow-employee] with having been at a Bawdy-House, which would be the Ruin of him in the End; he was much vex'd at her, and while he was at Dinner, the Devil enter'd so strongly into him, that he was resolv'd within himself to kill her: So when his Master and all the rest of the Family were gone to Church, leaving only the Maid and him at Home, he goes into the Bar and fetches a Hammer, with which knocking on the Billows as he sat by the Fire, the Maid chid him for making a Noise. He says nothing to her, but went to the Kitchen-Window and knockt there with the Hammer, at which the Maid then saying nothing at all, to provoke her, walks on the clean Dresser-Board with his dirty Shoes forwards and backwards several times together; which Piece of Malice incensing the Maid to scold at him, he suddenly threw the Hammer with such Violence at her, that hitting her on the head, she presently fell down shrieking; then he went and took up the Hammer, and laid it down again twice, not daring to strike her any more; but at last taking it up the third time, the Devil was so great with him, that he gave her many Blows with all the Force he could, and quickly dispatch'd her out of the World.   (qtd. in Richetti, 53-54)

This chilling account certainly dwells on the abhorrent nature of the crime, but its main effect is to induce horror and dread in the reader. Identification with the criminal is actually discouraged: his behaviour is inhuman and impenetrable. The eighteenth-century habit of reading collectively should surely be borne in mind here: one imagines groups of friends and family members gathering around the hearth to read this story aloud together, trembling in the consciousness of their vulnerability to brutal attackers.

Twentieth-century critical analyses of eighteenth-century fictional realism may, by stressing Watt's notion that realism is "only a convention,"[19] encourage us to forget the extent to which early realist narratives exploited their readers' direct experiences and aroused their strongest emotions. Such realism was not the product of clinical experiments with literary form, nor was it merely a reaction against the universalizing, idealizing tendencies of "aristocratic romance."[20] It was realism for the sake of sensationalism, even if sensation sometimes threatened to propel the reader into a world of improbable Gothic violence. As J. Paul Hunter puts it,

> When available, personal confessions of horrible conduct were preferred by publishers to simple accounts of the events, apparently because such statements seemed to finesse the issue of authenticity while often providing vivid, immediate, and convincing detail.[21]

Realism, in other words, was sought from a desire to make literature correspond to the readers' own lives—a point which would probably seem self-evident to any non-professional reader today. Those critics who do pay attention to context, notably Lincoln B. Faller,[22] have indeed noted the obsession of early crime writers with both the depravity of their subjects and the horrifying threat they posed to ordinary citizens.

To recapitulate: there are a number of reasons for understanding *Moll Flanders* as an intervention in the contemporary debate about crime. Firstly, it makes overt attempts to persuade the reader to recognize the folly of the victims of crime—the baronet Moll finds at Smithfield, for example. Second, it was published at a time when there was a perceived rise in crime, especially against property. Third, it explicitly presents itself as belonging to the sub-genres of rogue and whore biographies, which typically tried to frighten and appall their readers. The fourth reason, which is yet to be considered, is that Defoe offers his novel as an explanation for the criminal behaviour of certain individuals, implying that Moll is typical of women in her socio-economic position. For all the novel sets out to make us lock our doors and keep a close eye on our valuables, it simultaneously conveys a great deal of sympathy for the criminal, and forces us to recognize her, too, as a victim.

This function of the narrative is not immediately apparent from Defoe's preface, which constitutes powerful evidence for supposing an ironic distance between the author and the heroine. Its tone is fastidious:

> It is true that the original of this story is put into new words, and the style of the famous lady we here speak of is a little altered; particularly she is made to tell her own tale in modester words than she told it at first, the copy which came first to hand having been written in language more like one still in Newgate than one grown penitent and humble, as she afterwards pretends to be. (218)

For some readers, of course, the rest of the preface undermines this claim to detachment, since the pious tone of the "editor" rapidly gives way to excitement as he discusses Moll's history. Sanctimony undoubtedly invites scepticism when it is prefaced to a narrative whose content is salacious; and I would not wish to deny that Defoe was capable of disingenuousness when it came to defending the more populist of his works. In a sense *Moll Flanders* capitalizes on the very sins it attempts to excoriate. But Defoe was surely justified in drawing attention to the ways in which Moll's story serves as a warning, firstly to the honest victims of crime, and secondly to the young who might be tempted into it. On the one hand Moll's "robbing a little innocent child, dressed fine by the vanity of the mother, to go to the dancing-school, is," as Defoe says, "a good memento to such people hereafter, as is likewise her picking the gold watch from the young lady's side in the Park" (30-31), but on the other hand the narrative demonstrates repeatedly that Moll's misdeeds are a consequence of social and economic deprivation. Unlike the murderer whose horrific story was quoted above, Moll is an object of pity as well as disapprobation, and even the sententious preface hints that what she does is largely explained by her circumstances:

> When a woman debauched from her youth, nay, even being the offspring of debauchery and vice, comes to give an account of all her vicious practices, and even to descend to the particular occasions and circumstances by which she first became wicked, and of all the progression of crime which she ran through in threescore years, an author must be hard put to it to wrap it up so clean as not to give room, especially for vicious readers, to turn it to his disadvantage. (28)

We should not, however, misinterpret Defoe's emphasis on Moll's culpability; it stems from a realistic view of human nature rather than a sentimental one. His subsequent plea for the Virginia colonies as a solution to crime might sound like moral latitude, but it reflects a humanitarianism which is ultimately pragmatic. He wants society to respond to crime more intelligently and effectively than current legislation allowed (ironically, the punitive Black Act passed by Parliament in the following year would make things worse, not better).[23] That Moll is acknowledged to be less of a penitent than she would like us to think is not a sign of Defoe's inability to resist her, though he certainly feels some sympathy for her, but of his belief in the need to deal with her kind constructively. His novel will, therefore, build up a convincing psychological profile of a woman who turns to prostitution and theft, allowing us to view her from the inside and not simply as a faceless threat to the social fabric.

The openings of *Memoirs of a Cavalier* and *Captain Singleton* have taught us to pay close attention to Defoe's play with biographical conventions in his fictional histories (see also *Colonel Jack*, below). In the case of *Moll Flanders*, the heroine introduces herself with all the self-assurance we would expect from a hardened convict, even slipping into cant when she describes the death which awaited her mother "by the steps and the string" (33). Having identified herself as coming from criminal stock, she reminds us that orphans in France are rescued and educated by the state, in contrast to the plight of English infants like herself. Defoe is characteristically double-edged here: though Moll's tone is self-pitying and manipulative, she does have a point (that Defoe was strongly committed to state care for orphaned children is amply demonstrated in *Colonel Jack*). He clearly wants to make us feel regret for Moll's early hardships, as well as to mock her capacity for righteous self-justification. As she says, many girls similarly abandoned fell into prostitution and venereal disease which, as she spells out, "in its ordinary course tended to the swift destruction both of soul and body" (34). The reference alerts us to the near certainty that she will find herself forced to become a whore, and Defoe is determined his readers should attribute this in large part to her background.

Moll tells us that her mother was convicted of a felony, and that she had no father. Given Defoe's tendency to place an almost atavistic weight on the circumstances of his protagonists' births, her subsequent fortunes as a thief are easy to predict. (The Cavalier's mother dreamt of armies during pregnancy, which was enough to ensure that her son would grow up to be a soldier.) In *The Spectator* (1711-12) Addison and Steele had satirized the enthusiasm of contemporary biographers for mysterious signs and portents, Mr Spectator introducing himself with the "Story" in his family, "that when my Mother was gone with Child of me about three Months, she dreamt that she was brought to Bed of a Judge."[24] On the evidence of Moll's story, Defoe was clearly less cynical, though one of his prejudices at least was shared by Mr Spectator. In a subsequent paper the latter dwelt on the habits of gypsies, explaining that they were prone to thieving, pickpocketing and lying.[25] That Defoe's Moll was brought up for a while by a group of gypsies presumably compounded her inherited tendency to crime.

Fortunately the gypsies left her behind in Colchester, a town which the *Tour through the Whole Island of Great Britain* would commend for its architecture, industry, and devotion to William III.[26] It also boasted two charity schools, according to the *Tour*, although Moll found herself placed with a parish nurse. She was well cared for, and given a religious education, but she was constantly afraid she would have to go into domestic service, and longed to be able to work for herself. Service was indeed the only reasonable option for girls such as Moll, and the implied negligence of the government in allowing this state of affairs is conveyed by Moll's discussion with her nurse. As the nurse intimates, the only way a poor woman without friends could earn her living was through prostitution; indeed, "work" itself was evidently a morally ambiguous term for women,[27] and so was "gentlewoman."

Moll's upbringing, in short, preordains her to the life of a whore and thief, and though it may be impossible to tell where Defoe's sense of providential determination leaves off and his belief in the importance of environmental conditioning begins, this novel, like *Colonel Jack*, takes care not to place sole blame on its protagonist for turning to crime. Like *Memoirs of a Cavalier* and *Captain Singleton*, it is divided into two main sections; the first focuses on Moll's economic status as a young, marriageable woman, and the second on her economic status as a post-menopausal widow.

Previous readers have noted Defoe's preoccupation with necessity as the motive for crime. Quoting the *Review* of 15 September 1711, Bram Dijkstra observes that "in Defoe's eyes it was virtually a law of nature that 'Men rob for Bread' while 'Women whore for Bread.' "[28] Dijkstra extrapolates from this to suggest that Roxana takes the only appropriate course of action when she becomes a courtesan. Though this reading ignores Roxana's subsequent misery and self-condemnation (and the moral force behind the use of the verb "whore" in the *Review*), there is, as we shall see, considerable merit in the idea that *Moll Flanders* is, to some extent at least, about the dire options available firstly to a poor young woman, and then to a poor old one.

Moll appears to have found a solution to friendless poverty and female dependency when she joins the household of the town's mayor; all she is expected to do is sew and entertain the ladies of the family. But sewing, as she has already been told, will never give her a living, and as soon as she passes puberty she is expected to earn her keep with her only material possession, her body. The elder brother begins by flattering her, and the blame for what ensues is just as much his as Moll's, if not more. He seduces her with a few guineas—to her they represent a small fortune—impregnates, and then discards her. That his father is a prominent public figure, and his own wealth considerable, makes his conduct all the more reprehensible, and it is noted that he gets her away in the first place by sending her out to buy "two fine neckcloths," sufficient indication of his vanity and shallowness. (One recalls the embroidered waistcoat which Richardson's Pamela was asked to make for Mr. B.)

Though the greater share of the blame rests with her lover, for Moll this early lapse makes all the subsequent ones inevitable: "thus I finished my own destruction at once" (51), she says, reflecting the still-popular belief, corroborated by criminal psychologists, that succumbing to one temptation weakens a subject's resistance to the next. Yet when the family's younger son falls in love with her she makes every effort (at first) to extricate herself. She has a clear sense of right and wrong, and is particularly disturbed by the idea of incest. Defoe reserves much of his condemnation of the marriage for the younger brother, who refuses to acknowledge the duty he owes his parents. We can only guess at the extent to which this section of the novel reflects Defoe's own fears as a father at the time of writing; in 1722 his sons Benjamin and Daniel were of an age to be at risk from just such temptations. Every parent's worst fears are borne out when the younger brother leaves Moll a widow, and she promptly absconds, leaving their two children with her in-laws. The unmistakable moral of this episode is not that Defoe's readers should avoid a life of whoring and deceit—he shows that Moll behaved badly because she had little choice in the matter—but that they should watch out when employing young female servants lest their sons should go astray.

The narrative continues to focus as much on the weaknesses of human nature in general as on the faults of Moll in particular. Her second marriage reflects the fact that she now puts "no small value on [herself]" (77); since her husband is a linen-draper she can look forward with justification to a life of comfort. Unfortunately, however, she still nurses her childish aspirations to gentility, and the linen-draper is not a steady tradesman but an "amphibious creature," "a gentleman tradesman" (78). Such men were frequent targets for Defoe's satire. Moll's new husband wears a sword and dresses like a gentleman; and while Richetti may be putting it a little strongly when he suggests that this sword is supposed to represent "aristocratic sexuality,"[29] there is a sense in which the linen-draper's dress does suggest the upper-class Restoration beau who was anathema to a puritanical citizen like Defoe. In *The Complete English Tradesman* (1726), for example, a sword and a wig betoken an unsteady, frivolous temperament in a tradesman.[30]

Fine clothes, as Colonel Jack's suit of green reminds us, could also signal one's political allegiance. G. L. Apperson explains why:

> The beau of the Restoration era was a tremendous creature. He wore the fullest and most flowing of wigs; from his wrist hung the dandiest of clouded canes; and in his hand he flourished the never-failing snuff-box. At every step his wig and clothes and daintily-laced handkerchief exhaled the most delicate perfumes. The finest lace adorned his cravat and the cuffs of his coat; and, by a refinement of effeminacy, the same expensive trimming fringed the full and be-ribboned petticoat-breeches which Charles II and his courtiers brought to this country from the Court of Versailles.[31]

Commentators have noticed how, in nineteenth-century fiction, a male character's moral qualities are encoded in the way he drives his carriage (thus Mr. Knightley drives with exaggerated care; Alec D'Urberville recklessly). For Defoe and his sympathetic readers a predisposition to finery must have been an indelible sign of High Toryism. "Vanity," says Moll tartly, "is the perfection of a fop" (79). The linen-draper breaks all the rules of a good English tradesman,[32] wasting his capital on a fancy coach, expensive liveries and a trip to Oxford, and he ends up in a sponging-house, the fate of many a dissipated character in eighteenth-century fiction. Not surprisingly, Moll is very relieved when he flees to France and is never to be heard of again. Defoe's readers are to take heed: men can be just as vain and extravagant as women.

At this point Moll mentions parenthetically that the only child from this marriage is dead, an indication of callousness which has repulsed many critics and which is also somewhat at odds with her passionate outburst following her reunion with one of her sons in Virginia towards the end of the narrative. The momentary callousness and the subsequent display of "normal" maternal feeling may both be explained, however. On the one hand Defoe constructs Moll as a stereotypical whore who has no interest in the consequences of her promiscuity and the helpless offspring with which she burdens society. On the other hand he wants his readers to acknowledge the hardship which leads women to behave as Moll does, and to understand that her conduct often does make her miserable. The law forbids her to re-marry, even though her husband has abandoned her, and she therefore has no choice but to follow him into the Mint, where she is undoubtedly much better off childless. (The reference to the Mint is topical, too; as the Norton editor points out, it would be abolished as a sanctuary for debtors in 1723, having become the haunt of criminals.)[33]

Moll is not a genuine debtor herself, since she has saved around £500 from her marriage, and she has no difficulty in earning her keep by entertaining the male debtors. Her account of them is clearly intended to evoke the Restoration libertines who filled the Inns of Court in Defoe's own youth; she makes explicit reference to John Wilmot, Earl of Rochester, for example, and exactly captures the spirit of ennui and self-destruction which characterized the late seventeenth-century epicurean:

> There was something horrid and absurd in their way of sinning, for it was all a force even upon themselves; they did not only act against conscience, but against nature; they put a rape upon their temper to drown the reflections, which their circumstances continually gave them; and nothing was more easy than to see how sighs would interrupt their songs, and paleness and anguish sit upon their brows, in spite of the forced smiles they put on; nay, sometimes it would break out at their very mouths when they had parted with their money for a lewd treat or a wicked embrace.   (82)

Again Defoe's moral disgust is prompted less by Moll than the world around her. She is so appalled by these libertines that she leaves the Mint on the invitation of a friend who shares her desire to re-visit the marriage market. She finds the London approach to matrimony shockingly mercenary, however; as she says, it bears out the view of her Colchester sister-in-law that "money only made a woman agreeable" (83). Both Maximillian Novak and Shirlene Mason point out that Defoe is consistent in defending love-matches, and that he does so explicitly in *Conjugal Lewdness*.[34]

Moll's emotive language reveals his sense that marriages based exclusively on money are sinful:

> men chose mistresses indeed by the gust of their affection, and it was requisite to a whore to be handsome, well-shaped, have a good mien and a graceful behaviour; but that for a wife, no deformity would shock the fancy,

no ill qualities the judgement; the money was the thing; the portion was neither crooked nor monstrous, but the money was always agreeable, whatever the wife was. (83-84)

Subsequent pages describe some of the "tricks" (88) which determined women used to deceive rich men into marriage, but again Defoe's irony is not solely at Moll's expense. Both sexes behave dishonestly in the struggle to make an advantageous match. Moll commends her friend's skill in raising her value in her lover's eyes, reminding us that, at a time when relatively high numbers of women were unmarried, Defoe shared the concern for women's status of early feminist writers such as Mary Astell.[35] Like Moll, he saw "no necessity" (89) for women's self-denigration. As he showed, they could be as sharp and calculating as men when it came to courtship and marriage.

In fact Moll proves the winner on this occasion, having convinced a Virginia planter that she has a substantial fortune. He is disappointed when he eventually discovers she has so little, but comforted that she has some money at least, and eventually persuades her to go to Virginia with him. Defoe's belief in the colonies as the solution to poverty for both the nation and individual men and women was, as I have said, a recurrent theme in his fiction and, despite a dreadful voyage and an attack by pirates, Moll arrives safely in Virginia and lives very happily there. Her mother-in-law rhapsodizes about the opportunities for self-advancement offered to ex-transports after their seven years have been served: some have even become justices and magistrates, she says.

All would have been well, had Moll not discovered that her mother-in-law was her mother, and the planter, therefore, her brother. She flees from Virginia, less because she is horrified than because she can never hope to re-marry there. Critical accounts of *Moll Flanders* often insist on the heroine's material success through all the exigencies which confront her, but her narrative actually emphasizes her increasing desperation at this and other moments. Here, for example, she comments that "a new scene of misfortunes attended me, which perhaps few women have gone through the like of" (115).

She heads for Bath, a city notorious for sexual licence throughout the eighteenth century, and one where it will be easy for her to meet a range of possible suitors. The initially chaste relationship she forms with a gentleman she meets there provides another occasion for implicit moralizing, for the gentleman has a wife living, though she is insane. Insanity being inadequate grounds for divorce, he is, to all intents and purposes, forced into adultery, and his resolution to lie chastely with

Moll is, as one might expect, shortlived. His initial scruples indicate a fundamentally virtuous nature, though unfortunately for Moll they also mean that he subsequently casts her off in an agony of guilt. In addition, since he is already married she is never able to entertain hopes of marrying him, a disadvantage underscored by his generosity when she becomes pregnant. Moll can afford to indulge her maternal feelings to an unprecedented degree when this child arrives, but she is unable to support him, or to live as another man's mistress while he is with her. She is therefore obliged to send him to a nurse, whereupon, single and unencumbered again, she reckons up her stock and discovers she has much the same as before: around £450. She has no friends whatever, though, a much greater problem for a woman than a man, since, as she says, women are particularly vulnerable to thieves, fraudsters and cheating goldsmiths.

Again Defoe is careful to stress that his heroine's plight is a common one for unmarried women; Moll had the potential to be a faithful wife, he says, but had no hope of meeting a "sober, good husband" (135). Men are therefore shown to suffer in their turn from the neglect of women, since Moll has at least three other partners in the course of her peregrinations and none benefits from his involvement with her. The first is an honest clerk who treats Moll with respect but finally explains he has a wife who is cuckolding him, Defoe's point being that not all women who end up like Moll have her excuse. That she refuses to find similarities between this wife's story and her own does not suggest Defoe is indulging her, but rather the reverse: it is further evidence of her habituation to whoredom. But when she notes that it is necessary "for all women who expect anything in the world, to preserve the character of their virtue, even when perhaps they may have sacrificed the thing itself" (144), his main target is not his cynical heroine but society at large, which prizes reputation above true virtue.

Her greed increasing, Moll next jeopardizes an offer of marriage from the same clerk in order to try her hand in a new market, the north west. There she displays the tolerance towards Catholicism which characterizes so many of Defoe's morally dubious protagonists, and is rewarded by being duped into marriage with a poor man. The man himself is taken in, believing Moll rich, but he is almost the only one of her husbands for whom she expresses strong affection. In eighteenth-century terms he is a fit companion for a professional whore, as he turns out to be a notorious highwayman.

He leaves her pregnant but—as she soon realises—married status means very little to a pregnant woman on her own: "whether I was a whore or a wife, I was to pass for a whore" (164). In desperation she finds herself a midwife who has sheltered dozens of pregnant women, rich and poor, from discovery. Once again Defoe is less interested in Moll's lack of honesty about herself than in her function as an emblem for an age of promiscuity. The episode in the midwife's house reveals glimpses of a shadowy world of abortion and infanticide which embraces the highest and the lowest in the land; as Moll remarks, the experience "was a strange testimony of the growing vice of the age" (170).

At last she is re-united with her honest clerk, the midwife readily talking her out of her scruples about bigamy. She is punished for the deceit when she has an embarrassing near-encounter with the highway-men on her honeymoon, but from that moment her life promises to be more comfortable and virtuous than ever before, her new husband having little knowledge of her chequered past.

This husband, the clerk, earns Defoe's approval on every count. He is sober and "sensible," virtuous and industrious. He is modestly well-off, but not rich enough to support an extravagant lifestyle. Moll passes five happy years with him, until he suffers sudden huge losses from a borrower and lacks the strength of mind required to recover his spirits. When he dies, Moll is forty-eight; as she says, "past the flourishing time ... when [she] might expect to be courted for a mistress" (187). She has no women friends to support her in her terror and grief, and spends two miserable years alone while her money ebbs away. She appeals directly to the reader for sympathy and forgiveness when she turns to stealing, a device Defoe commonly uses to jolt his readers into understanding those who take to crime. "Let them remember that a time of distress is a time of dreadful temptation, and all the strength to resist is taken away; poverty presses, the soul is made desperate by distress, and what can be done?" (188-89), asks Moll rhetorically. She is out of her senses, she says, when she commits her first theft, so it cannot really be said to have been premeditated. Again Defoe's attitude to her is ambiguous: she is seen to make every excuse for herself, but the excuses have, after all, a degree of justification given Moll's physical and social circumstances.

Her first theft is a bundle of expensive child-bed linen, a sad reminder of the days when she could legitimately afford such luxuries. Her distress, however, arises mainly from imagining the suffering of her victim, and is short-lived. Within a few days she goes out again, and this time finds a little child on its way home from dancing-school. In the preface Defoe singled out this episode as one of special significance, serving as it did to warn parents against carelessly exposing their chil-dren to thieves. That the child has been to dancing-class wearing a fine gold necklace suggests that her parents are inordinately vain and, moreover, overly fond of French fashions (dancing is one of the accomplishments Colonel Jack learns in France and considers vital to his education as a gentleman).

Moll justifies herself for the theft of the necklace with the thought that she has given the parents a "just reproof for their negligence in leaving the poor little lamb to come home by itself." The self-deception is psychologically plausible, as well as perfectly consistent with a sincere desire on Defoe's part to rebuke those who pay more attention to their children's appearance than to their personal safety. His *Review* carried a number of advertisements for children whose families had lost them; Moll was herself stolen as a small child by gypsies, and Captain Singleton was kidnapped at the age of two when his nursemaid left him playing outside a public house near Islington Fields. The account of Moll's flight with the necklace through a maze of lanes and passages underscores the dangers to children from London's dark alleys. Moll constructs a frightening scenario in which the girl's mother could not resist dressing her up, then left her in the care of a maid who was distracted by "some fellow that had met her by the way" (192). Moll may sound hypocritical, but Defoe must have shared her contempt for Londoners who lacked the sense to look after their children.

The street-names which feature in the second section of the novel emphasize that most of Moll's crimes take place in the old city, bordered by Clerkenwell and Moorfields to the north, Lincoln's Inn Fields to the west, and Whitechapel to the east. Defoe is anxious for his urban readers to recognize the setting for the heroine's adventures and understand that they are at risk from thieves just like her. Ultimately he suggests that all Londoners are vulnerable to crime: Moll's activities centre at first on the old city, but eventually encompass Covent Garden, the Strand, the Mall and Knightsbridge. When the summer weather sends the population away, she goes to rural Essex, which gives her plenty of opportunities for cheating inn-keepers and robbing travellers of their belongings.

In the first section of her narrative Moll had explained how she became involved with successive men from all walks of life, from gentlemen's sons to tradesmen-dandies to honest clerks and men of substantial property. Her victims in the second section are just as diverse, ranging from the wealthiest to the poorest in society, and she steals everything she finds, from lace to jewellery to clothing. With this Defoe appears to conform to the conventions of criminal biographers; Captain Alexander Smith's *Lives of the Most Noted Highway-men, Foot-pads, House-*

breakers, Shoplifts, and Cheats of Both Sexes (1714), for example, places the same emphasis on the alarming range and versatility of contemporary criminals (see Kelly 298-304). It is doubly alarming that Moll eventually evades justice, though presumably it was what contemporaries would have expected. No doubt rates of conviction have always seemed low in proportion to the number of reported offences.

All the evidence, then, points to reading *Moll Flanders* as a cautionary tale aimed at those whose carelessness makes crime so profitable as well as an examination of the factors driving some women to crime. Defoe's attitude to his heroine is mixed. He presents her as an undoubted menace to society, but also indicts society for failing to protect itself from people like her, and for producing her in the first place. Her many brazen attempts to exonerate herself are ironic in two ways, illustrating the criminal's refusal to take responsibility for his or her actions, and revealing our complacency in ignoring the dangers which stare us in the face. Moll's extraordinary successes show just how easy it is for someone to steal from under their victims' very noses.

By insisting that we recognise the straightforwardly homiletic tone of the narrative I do not, therefore, diminish its subtlety or contradict its claims to complexity. Defoe meant us to be afraid of Moll, but sorry for her too; after all, her pleas for mercy are consonant with the views on crime and punishment expressed in the *Review* and *Colonel Jack*. Defoe himself had spent time in Newgate, and there is undeniable poignancy in the account of Moll's imprisonment there. Moreover, in the early eighteenth century, the "prerogative of mercy," argues Hay, "ran throughout the administration of the criminal law, from the lowest to the highest level" (157), and it would have had particular meaning for Defoe as a lifelong opponent of absolutism. His life of Jonathan Wild, published in 1725, features a woman who would rather lose her jewelled watch than have someone hanged for stealing it,[36] and elsewhere in his work he associates harsh punishment with recidivism and brutalization. Nowhere does he propose the usual eighteenth-century answers to crime: an increase in the number of capital offences, or an expansion of the prison population.

In a sense it is ironic that some critics have seen Moll as an economic individualist, for hers is a poignantly commonplace story, and she has no unique qualities—quite the opposite. Defoe wants her to stand for a whole sub-stratum of society, the women who turn to crime because they were neglected as children and lack financial security in adulthood. Her name has often attracted attention since it recalls both Moll Cut-purse, the pseudonym of Mary Frith, and Moll King, the associate of Jonathan

Wild on whom Gerald Howson argues Defoe based his heroine.[37] "Moll" is, of course, a generic name for a prostitute and a female thief, but "Moll Flanders" is both generic and metonymic, "Flanders" signalling Moll's taste for purloining expensive Flanders lace, just as the name of Jonathan Wild's second wife, "Mrs Milliner," associated her with a profession which bordered on prostitution,[38] or as "Callico Sarah" indicated that person's propensity for contraband Indian cloth.[39] "Moll Flanders" is not a realistic name, then, whether or not some individuals in real life happened to share it. It is, like Captain Bob Singleton, Colonel Jack or Roxana, a name which identifies the protagonist with a recognisable, rather alarming contemporary type. The novel shows us why some women turn to prostitution and stealing, and ultimately, perhaps, it is as interested in implying the need for social reforms as in recommending practical measures for outwitting the resourceful criminal mind.

CHAPTER FOUR

"I was a kind of an Historian": The Productions of History in *Colonel Jack*

This study is based on the premise that all Defoe's novels were shaped first and foremost by their political and historical circumstances, but *Colonel Jack*[1] is perhaps one of those most densely packed with references to recent history. Its historical allusiveness may account for its relative critical neglect in the twentieth century by comparison with *Robinson Crusoe* or *Moll Flanders*, as well as for the recent slight rise in its critical fortunes.[2] However, we are justified in describing it as a historical novel less by its supposed generic identity than by its guiding assumption that history is both the producer and the product of the human subject. *Colonel Jack* exemplifies the concern with the relationship between the individual and society which I have argued characterizes most of Defoe's novels and which accounts for the complexity of their ironic strategies. As this chapter hopes to show, it is the most extended demonstration of Defoe's belief that the individual (especially the historiographer) can and does influence the world of public events.

If we take the narrator at face value, the novel offers a relatively conventional and simplistic historical model in which the individual is a victim of forces beyond his or her control. Yet we are continually encouraged to question Jack's veracity, and hence to recognize the contribution the individual makes to the course of history. Although Jack would like the reader to subscribe to the first model, since this would absolve him of responsibility for his many crimes and deceits, his narrative nonetheless reveals his agency—his direct and conscious role in the creation of his times. But Defoe does not indicate that the first model should be replaced with one equally mechanistic. Ultimately *Colonel Jack* suggests that historical epochs or societies and those who live in them are mutually determined.

We can call this view materialist, and not simply because it insists on the relationship between the individual and society as non-accidental, specific and susceptible to analysis, but also because it regards economics as the fundamental determinant of social relationships. Defoe's hero is consistently motivated by the desire to own more money and things, though his abiding tendency is to deny, ignore or conceal the means of acquisition. It is Defoe's aim to expose this material reality, and to satirize the tone of sententious justification commonly adopted by those who wish to conceal their self-interestedness. Jack, like the Cavalier, Singleton, or Moll Flanders, is on the make, and while Defoe does not necessarily object to the ends, he does find himself alarmed by the means.

Jack wants it both ways, in fact, for although his "Memoirs" (307) are an extended plea for understanding and forgiveness on the basis that he could not help his various misdemeanours, he frequently demonstrates his consciousness of the implications of his conduct, and indeed regards his role in the momentous events of European history as compelling and important. His restlessness in Virginia derives from a belief that he is missing out on the main action, Defoe vividly conveying the frustration felt by a planter cut off from the world of newsprint and gossip in Jack's description of his eye-opening friendship with an educated convict:

> He read History to me, and where Books were wanting, he gave me Ideas of those things which had not been Recorded by our modern Histories, or at least, that our Number of Books would not reach; by these things he rais'd an unquenchable Thirst in me, after seeing something that was doing in the World. (171-72)

Jack clearly shares his creator's belief in the power of texts to alter readers and hence society, and the prefatory claim by the "editor," albeit perhaps tongue-in-cheek, that *"Every wicked Reader will here be encouraged to a Change"* (2), is echoed by Jack's urging "all that design to read it" to "prepare to do so with the Temper of Penitents" (308). He believes his "History may find a place in the World" (3), and indeed the text begins with an implicit analogy between its own entrance into the world and the hero's birth. Coming into the world remains Jack's chief concern, whether in terms of the transformation from criminal to law-abiding citizen, in the literal voyage from colonial to Londoner, or in the readmission of the rebel into the dominant political order. His "Memoirs" constitute an additional gesture towards integration, marking the various stages (and reversals) of his rehabilitation and asserting his social and political importance, and there is an unmistakable parallel here with Defoe's own political aspirations. Even if we are encouraged to smile at Jack's less than modest claims to have played prominent roles in a number of key military campaigns and political uprisings in the first two decades of the eighteenth century, we are nonetheless conscious of him as a significant historical figure and of Defoe's text as a social and political commentary which is optimistic about its own potential to influence history.

In what follows I shall consider first, Defoe's enlightened presentation of his hero as the product of social deprivation in childhood and early adulthood; then his exposure of this hero's attempts to disown responsibility for his conduct; and lastly the still more enlightened recognition, implicit in the text, that history is simultaneously the product and producer of human agents. As we shall see, all three approaches to history—whether as a source or consequence of human errors (and successes) or both—are ideologically and politically motivated, being used to support Defoe's objections to Catholicism, Jacobitism and the ascendancy of France, and to reflect his concern with certain social evils: inadequate state education; childhood poverty; crime; institutional brutality in England, Scotland and the colonies. All this forms a broad but unified critique, for these social ills are seen as intimately bound up with the sectarian and political divisions inherited from the mid-seventeenth century.

Defoe's overtly didactic responses to certain social abuses should be dealt with first, since to some extent he does exonerate Jack for his part in various crimes and blame the state for its dereliction of duty. For example, in lamenting the absence of state provision for the care and education of orphans, he endorses the hero's presentation of his crimes as the consequence of social neglect. In the preface the "editor" gives official sanction to the rationale Jack invariably offers for his behaviour, articulating exactly the same opinion which Jack puts so colloquially: "As for your humble Servant, Colonel Jack, he was a poor unhappy tractable Dog, willing enough, and capable too, to learn any thing, if he had had any but the Devil for his School-Master" (6). Necessity as the motive for crime (a theme common to Defoe's writings on theft and prostitution) is a virtual refrain in Jack's narrative, applied not only to himself (e.g. 156) but to others, such as the cultivated gentleman who is forced to turn highwayman and narrowly misses the gallows (161), and the impoverished gentlewoman who goes on the streets (232).[3]

According to the Preface, the answer to ridding England of its swollen population of juvenile offenders is an overhaul of the state education system ("*publick Schools, and Charities*" [1]), since a decent education would obviate the need for children to embark on a life of crime.[4] *Colonel Jack* has been viewed by some critics as a serious contribution to contemporary debates on educational issues,[5] and the hero is certainly conscious that his lack of education is his chief disadvantage in his efforts to make an honest living: "I had no Foundation lay'd in me by Education; and being early led by my fate into Evil, I had the less Sense of its being Evil left upon my Mind" (61). In one moment of sincere repentance he laments having lost not only his parents but the opportunities they would have given him to follow "some Trade, or Employment" (83). As soon as he can he learns to read and write, skills with which he is able to get a paid job (103), and he continues with his education in Virginia, becoming a lover of books (157).

His direct appeals to his readers to consider a reform of state education are matched by equally serious and explicit calls for an overhaul of the penal system, and *Colonel Jack* provides us with an unusually detailed account of transportation in the early eighteenth century.[6] Jack is not, of course, a typical contemporary transport, since he has evaded actual conviction (though not punishment) for his crimes, and his description of Virginia is supposedly set in the 1680s and 1690s.[7] But his narrative is probably best read in the context of the early 1720s, when Walpole's ministry was increasing drastically the number of capital crimes on the statute books.[8] Judging by his novels, Defoe favoured more humane solutions to the perceived crime wave: baldly stated proposals for an expansion of the transportation system punctuate *Moll Flanders* as well as *Colonel Jack*. Since criminals would have no need to offend if only they were skilled enough to find legitimate employment, in Jack's view the colonies will soon transform the desperate and disaffected into productive and honest citizens. He gives a concrete demonstration of the benefits of transportation himself, rising over the years from bonded servant to overseer to plantation owner, and leaving Virginia with an annual income of £400 to £600 derived from tobacco exports (233).

It is apparent from the precision with which Jack describes this process that Defoe was hopeful of converting his readers to a positive view of transportation, and that he genuinely regarded it as a means of rehabilitation rather than permanent exclusion. Related to both education and transportation is the subject of corporal punishment, and here, too, Jack's views are expressed plainly and repeatedly and, we may suppose, in accordance with those of Defoe himself. Whipping is a leitmotif of Jack's youth, his first traumatic experience as a child being not the death of his only adult protector, a misfortune he greets with equanimity, but his witnessing his foster-brother's whipping at Bridewell, a sight which "frighted [him] almost to Death" (12). It haunts him, so that when, on a subsequent occasion, he thinks he has lost all his money his reaction recalls this primal, horrific scene: "I came away in dispair, crying, and roaring like a little Boy that had been whip'd" (25). On another occasion, when faced with the possibility of arrest, he cannot rid himself of the frightening memory of his brother's cruel whipping (28), and his friend Will exploits his fear in order to silence his objections to their theft of some bills (30). The foster-brother himself is mentally scarred by his whipping, the sight of two criminals being scourged in the streets of Edinburgh reminding him "of what he had suffer'd, when he was but a Boy; at the famous place, call'd *Bridewell*" (100). Whipping as an image of agony and shame is so central to Jack's consciousness that years later he describes caning his wife's lover "till he roar'd out like a Boy soundly whipt" (243).

These references are neither gratuitous nor casual but have a serious function in reinforcing Defoe's arguments for crime prevention through state education for the poorest and humane methods of correction: in essence, transportation. His opposition to corporal punishment is humanitarian but also practical: however appalled by the threat of Bridewell, Jack was not deterred from crime by it. His experiences as a thief are interspersed with horrified references to his likely fate, but he continues to steal anyway, while his foster-brother, Captain Jack, seems hardened rather than subdued by his beating.

The traditional punishment inflicted on juvenile delinquents has an obvious bearing on the subject of the colonies, since there too discipline is maintained by force, and there too, according to Defoe, corporal punishment is ineffective and morally repugnant. Jack's experiences in Virginia are partly designed to illustrate the benefits of using reason rather than violence in the management of slaves. A series of anecdotes about the value of extending mercy to slaves ends with this justification from Jack:

> I HAVE dwelt the longer upon it, that if possible Posterity might be persuaded to try gentler Methods with those miserable Creatures, and to use them with Humanity. (149-50)

The shift in focus from Jack's early experiences as a pickpocket to his subsequent life as a plantation overseer might at first sight seem to indicate Defoe's supposed propensity for narratives in which disparate topics are loosely, even arbitrarily, connected through the adventures of a fictional criminal. *Moll Flanders*, written in the same year as *Colonel Jack*, is a like blend of criminal biography and propaganda on behalf of transportation. But we have seen (from *Memoirs of a Cavalier*, for instance) that Defoe was capable of using a bipartite structure for rhetorical effect, and the parallels between Jack's London boyhood and his experiences in the New World are not coincidental. Bonded servitude in Virginia provides Jack with a training and an honest livelihood, possibilities which were never open to him in England or Scotland. And the same reasons for regarding corporal punishment as unsatisfactory in England and Scotland apply in the colonies. Jack draws attention to the ethical implications of his sudden elevation from criminal to overseer:

> This part [i.e., his responsibility for beating those beneath him] turn'd the very blood within my Veins, and I could not think of it with any temper; that I, who was but Yesterday a Servant or Slave like them, and under the Authority of the same Lash, should lift up my Hand to the Cruel Work, which was my Terror but the Day before.   (127-28)

The long discussion of corporal punishment on the plantations which follows bears a direct relationship to the preceding English section of the narrative. Just as the story of Jack's boyhood exposes the brutality and inefficacy of conventional forms of punishment in England, especially the corporal correction of young offenders, so the story of his years as an overseer is used to censure the colonial practice of whipping slaves. Given the text's earlier concern with whipping as both a valueless and an inhumane punishment, Jack's attempts to reform coercive methods on his Virginia plantation can be seen in two ways. On the one hand they are an implicit critique of the English penal code, and on the other they are supported by Jack's earlier firsthand testimony against the inutility of whipping child criminals. Dressed in his overseer's garb and furnished with a mount and a scourge, he is barely distinguishable from an English country gentleman whose dominion over animals seems inextricably linked to his authority over the poor:

> when I entered upon my Office, I had a Horse given me, and a long Horse-whip, like what we call in *England* a Hunting-whip; the Horse was to ride up and down all over the Plantation to see the Servants and *Negroes* did their Work.   (127)

England is constantly evoked in the discussion of plantation beatings, the practice of whipping slaves being associated with the English colonists above all others. Jack hastens to absolve his countrymen from the charge that they are inherently tyrannical and cruel (128), but the association of the English with whipping is later confirmed, first by the planter (145) and secondly when Jack alludes to the dreadful conditions of slaves in Barbados and Jamaica (149), both of which were English colonies in the late seventeenth and early eighteenth centuries. There is, too, a telling pun in the planter's question to Jack:

> did you really intend to Whip the poor *Negro* twice a day, for four Days together; *that is to say*, to Whip him to Death, for that would have been the *English* of it, and the End of it. (132)

It is impossible to ignore the implications of Jack's radical reply to the planter's appeal to custom as the justification for whipping slaves. Jack's language betrays that he is thinking about his native country, not just the colonies: "There are it may be Publick and *National* Mistakes and Errors in Conduct, and this is One" (135; emphasis added).

Despite Defoe's critique of the social circumstances that produce criminals, conveyed by his unwillingness to side with his protagonist, his attitude to Jack is fundamentally critical and sceptical—not unlike his attitude to Moll Flanders, in fact. While there is some authorial endorsement of Jack's views on humanitarian issues, the reader is frequently made to distrust him. Parts of Jack's account are as ambiguous, biased and incomplete as others are direct, ingenuous and well-meant; at times he urges social reforms with a good deal of passion and logic, but he is also capable of breathtaking dishonesties. Strangely, the effect of his reversals is not to discredit the more transparently didactic passages of his narrative—we never feel the need to doubt the arguments against whipping, for example. Yet when he follows one of his earnest digressions with an altogether less candid account of an incident in his life, Defoe does mean to call his integrity into question and does so, I would argue, to teach us a lesson about people of Jack's type.

Ultimately the novel seeks to show that rich, unscrupulous traders and reckless Jacobites, both of which are represented by the hero, are likely to appear honourable, truthful and moderate, but that their plausibility is exactly why we need to be able to recognize when they are trying to deceive us. Defoe's strategy in this novel is thus a variation on the one he uses in *Memoirs of a Cavalier*, where we found ourselves nodding in respectful agreement with the Cavalier's informed account of royalist ineptitude, forgetting the anti-Stuart bias of his creator. With the pious-sounding rogue Colonel Jack we are similarly lulled into a false sense of security but gradually realize that he is utterly untrustworthy, rather than, as was the Cavalier, possessed of inside information and therefore to be regarded as fundamentally reliable. Yet how do we become aware of the lies and evasions which pervade Jack's narration, and how are we led to re-examine the proposition that crime is environmentally conditioned, and the individual merely the victim of irresistible social and historical pressures? As in the other novels discussed in this study, Defoe's most important rhetorical tool is the irony with which he regards his protagonist and narrator.

The alert reader notices that despite all his many confessions of past wrongdoings, the hero constantly finds excuses for himself. In describing the moment when he first surrendered to peer pressure from an experienced pickpocket, for example, his language becomes almost ludicrously portentous and Miltonic:

> WELL, upon the perswasions of this Lad, I walk'd out with him, a poor innocent Boy, and (as I remember, my very Thoughts perfectly well) I had no Evil in my Intentions; I had never stolen any thing in my Life, . . . but the subtile Tempter baited his Hook for me. (19)

He uses similar words to describe his seduction by the first woman he marries:

> I began to be ensnared, I knew not how, or to what End; and was on a sudden so embarrass'd in my Thoughts about her, that like a Charm she had me always in her Circle; if she had not been one of the subtilest Women on Earth, she could never have brought me to have given myself the least Trouble about her. (187)

Even when he assaults his second wife he justifies himself ("you must consider me now in the Circumstances of a Man enrag'd" [230]), while his involvement in the Jacobite Rebellion of 1715 is the fault of a "*Romish* Priest" whose provocative talk "gave [him] no rest" (264). And his participation in the lucrative illegal trade with New Spain is presented as a natural and just response to unreasonable Spanish protectionism and barbarity (287).

In these instances Jack's embarrassment is both comic and revealing, inviting us to question his integrity. His explanations for his actions may temporarily deceive us; as he says, he "has a natural Talent of Talking" (7) which manages to convince at least one gentleman—though wrongly—of his decency (38), while later, in Virginia, he talks himself out of bondage (122-25). Yet since we are privileged to see what he does as well as what he says he does, we become frankly suspicious of him. While he writes indignantly of his ill treatment by society, he repeatedly demonstrates his lack of loyalty to anyone or anything, most notably, of course, the state itself. His reluctance to "go over a poor Musquetier into *Flanders*, to be knock'd on the Head at the Tune of Three and Six-pence a Week" (105) is, while understandable, hardly patriotic, so that it comes as little surprise later to find him indifferent to his country's vital trading interests in the war with France. Whig support for William III's wars against Louis XIV mainly derived from the desire to protect English merchant shipping,[9] but the fact that Jack's livelihood while in Virginia depends on his tobacco exports does nothing to incline him to the Whig point of view (which was, of course, Defoe's). On his way back to England he loses some goods to a French privateer, but his concern for his own property is far outweighed by his interest in privateering as a novel method of legal theft: "to give them their Due, they Fought bravely for it" (180). It is predictable that he passes through Ghent as an unconcerned sightseer while his countrymen are fighting King William's War against the Spanish, and that he later fights for William's rival, Louis XIV, against the Austrians in Italy.

His indifference to England's interests at these junctures is, of course, intended by Defoe to prepare the ground for his greater acts of treason during the Jacobite uprisings of 1708 and 1715. Jacobitism has been identified by previous critics as a central theme of the novel,[10] and I would argue that it is as important to this narrative as the royalist cause is to *Memoirs of a Cavalier*. What first draws it to the reader's attention is the hero's obsession with his identity as a gentleman, for by subjecting Jack's desire for gentlemanliness to ironic scrutiny, Defoe gradually reveals his political affinities as shallow, brash and inauthentic.[11]

There is, for instance, a telling disparity between Jack's violent reaction to perceived slurs on his honour (as, for example, when his wife's creditor pursues him for a bill [199-203]) and his mercenary concern for self over king and country. Moreover, his indifference to William III is not matched by any very profound commitment to his Stuart rivals; his involvement in the Jacobite uprisings is half-hearted, and although he fights for the Catholic cause in Europe, this is purely for personal gain.

Defoe's exposé of a typical Jacobite is, however, subtle, and depends on our perception that Jack's use of the term "honour" signifies no more than his avid longing for increased status. As he would have it, he was born a gentleman, and this is the explanation and justification of his striving to overcome the circumstances of his upbringing. He develops a solemn aversion to swearing when he learns it is ungentlemanly, and he likes to threaten his sexual rivals with challenges to duels. Yet the reader wonders if all this is not deeply suspect in the context of his life. It is noticeable that he is very reluctant actually to use the sword he sports (201), and his gentlemanliness is called into question in other ways. Can an illegitimate child who is quickly dispatched to a nurse seriously claim gentle birth? As a child Jack indulges himself with romantic fantasies about his parentage, but the reader forms no very admirable impression of a mother who "kept very good Company"—in other words, became a mistress to an upper-class rake—or a father who disposed of his son on the understanding that he "should not be seen or heard of" (3) again. And Jack's father is not the only Restoration rake in *Colonel Jack*; though Jack himself believes passionately in the moral superiority of gentlemen (e.g. 60, 62, 155), they repeatedly feature in the text as seducers and libertines. It is, for example, "a Gentleman of a great Estate in that Country who promised [Jack's fourth wife, Moggy] Marriage, and [after impregnating her] deserted her" (249), while three of Jack's marriages involve his cuckolding by "gentlemen" (201, 227, 224).

I would not wish to deny that in some instances the gentleman is presented in the text as the manly ideal, the antithesis of the rogue who preys on him. Jack regards his stirrings of conscience as indicators of his gentle birth, and in describing his younger foster-brother he provides an unexceptionable definition of the gentleman:

> he had a true Manly Courage, fear'd nothing, and could look Death in the Face, without any Hesitation; and yet if he had the Advantage, was the most generous and most compassionate Creature alive; he had native Principles of Gallantry in him . . . and in a Word, he wanted nothing but Honesty to have made him an excellent Man. (6)

Such a definition calls to mind Defoe's conduct book, *The Compleat English Gentleman* (1729), and shorter works such as *An Apology for the Army* (1715), in which he celebrates the virtues of the gentleman; and it need not be viewed ironically.

We do, however, register that "Major" Jack (the hero's younger foster-brother) failed to live up to the ideal in terms of honesty (as, evidently, did his philanderer father, a Major of the Guards [6]) and so too does Jack himself. For despite his oft-iterated belief in the moral superiority of gentlemen, the text more often than not associates them with vanity and deceit. In instancing early signs of his innate gentility Jack describes his boyhood passion for associating with "the better Sort," only to add the unconsciously ironic qualifier, "I mean, the better Sort of those that would Converse with a Beggar-boy" (10). His childish assumption that being a gentleman means having a warm pair of stockings and dry shoes (15) seems scarcely different from his fantasies in adulthood: "I Dream't of nothing but being a Gentleman Officer, as well as a Gentleman Soldier" (105). The sailor who kidnaps Jack and his fellow-deserters clearly knows what he is about when he allows them to overhear the flattering enquiry, "where are these honest gentlemen Soldiers . . . ?" (109). When Jack finally does fulfil his ambition, and gains a commission for lieutenant from no less a person than the king, his true motives for serving are unceremoniously admitted:

> I gain'd the Reputation of a good Officer, but I happen'd to be in some particular Posts too, by which I got somewhat that I lik'd much better, and that was a good deal of Money. (209)

That Jack views a gentleman as a person with money and social status rather than virtue is even more tellingly revealed in the constant association of the word "gentleman" with criminality in the first section of the novel. Early on, for example, Will tempts Jack to a life of thieving with seductive references to "Courtisie" and the assurance that "as we are Gentlemen, we always do very Honestly by one another" (42). Later he promises to bring Jack into "a brave Gang . . . where you shall see we shall all be Gentlemen" (59). Though he hesitates to accept Will's definition of what a gentleman means, Jack refers quite naturally to his fellow-robbers as "Gentlemen Rogues" (69), and does not seem to notice that their much-vaunted code of honour among thieves is rarely adhered to in fact. Will reneges on his promises on the very first occasion that Jack acts as his accomplice:

> he shar'd the Money very honestly with me, only at the end he told me, that tho' it was true, he promis'd me half, yet as it was the first time, and I had done nothing but look on, so he thought it was very well if I took a little less than he did. (22)

Jack seems to grow towards an understanding that Will's gentleman is a rather less lofty being than his own ("a Villain of a higher Degree than a Pick-pocket" [62]), yet his own notion of what constitutes gentlemanly conduct seems equally dubious. Being a gentleman sometimes seems to mean no more than the possession of certain social accomplishments, for he boasts of dancing and playing cards after learning in France "every thing that was needful, to make me . . . a Gentleman" (191). The reader might well look back over his career of tireless social advancement, marked as it is by a cheerful disregard for the morality of his actions, and view his father's prophecy with retrospective irony:

100

he did not doubt, he said, but that sometime or other the very hint would inspire me with Thoughts suitable to my Birth, and that I would certainly act like a Gentleman, if I believed myself to be so. (3)

Here Defoe seems to be invoking the humorous and slang uses of "gentleman," as in "gentleman of fortune" (pirate), "gentleman of the road" (highwayman), and Falstaff's "gentlemen of the shade" or thieves (*Henry IV*, Part 1, 1.2.26).

As the reader cannot help but be aware, Jack's longing to be a gentleman is what impels him both to petty crime and to the treasonable crime of Jacobitism, and it is the political ramifications of his tireless efforts at self-advancement that I now wish to explore in detail. Although Jack would have us believe that his ambition is a purely personal, even idiosyncratic matter, attention to the many incidental political and historical references embedded in his narrative reveals that Jack is not so much alienated from his times as he is exemplifying them.

The inconsistencies and discrepancies in his narration have been frequently noted by critics, most recently, perhaps, by Michael Boardman. For Boardman they are a sign of Defoe's ideological confusion which only gave way to a clarity of vision and purpose in *Roxana* (1724), his last novel.[12] I would argue the opposite, for while Jack's own story may be incomplete and self-contradictory, Defoe intended it should be. He continually subverts his narrator's authority not because he is uncertain of his own ideological position but in order to expose the flaws and contradictions of Jacobitism. Far from ramshackle and unstructured, *Colonel Jack* is a coherent and sustained attack on the moral condition of the nation, and it seeks to link the recent rise in crimes of property and violence with the resurgence of Jacobitism. In Defoe's eyes both were manifestations of the anarchy which had seemed to threaten England in the mid-seventeenth century and which continued to obsess many commentators after the Protestant accession. While Jack acknowledges few connections between his own history and his times, Defoe is determined that the reader will see how extensive they really are.

It is worth remembering that the Jacobite threat seemed as acute as ever when *Colonel Jack* was published (it preoccupied Walpole for much of his premiership, in fact).[13] The uprising of 1718 led by the Earl of Mar followed closely on that of 1715, demonstrating that there remained significant and potentially destabilizing opposition to the Hanoverian line. Moreover, in 1722 Francis Atterbury, the Bishop of Rochester, conspired with the Jacobites to organize an invasion from France to coincide with an uprising in London during George I's summer vacation in Hanover. News of the plot broke, however, in May, and Walpole rapidly turned it to his advantage by associating it with the Tories.[14]

It seems reasonable, given the evidence, to assume that the publication of *Colonel Jack* at the end of the year was opportunistic. I have already described Defoe's lifelong aversion to "Papists, Jacobites, and Enraged High Tories," a "Generation" whom his "Very Soul abhor[red],"[15] in previous chapters, and Jacobitism runs like a thread throughout Jack's story (as Blewett [95] points out, even his name was a slang term for "Jacobite"). His birth can be dated as roughly contemporaneous with James II's avowal of Catholicism in 1672 and the passing of the Test Act in 1673;[16] he says he was not yet ten years old when his nurse's husband died in the sinking of the *Gloucester* in 1682. This ship was carrying the Duke of York—later James II—when it foundered, and reminds the reader of James's unconstitutional resumption of the naval command in 1684.[17] Moreover, James's role in the *Gloucester* affair was controversial; Gilbert Burnet's *History of His Own Time* (1715), for example, represents him as much to blame for the incident.[18]

Jack's infant associations with the Catholic king are reinforced by his nurse's slur on one of the heroes of English Protestants in the seventeenth century, the Duke of Monmouth. The nurse assures Jack that she has "known Colonels come to be Lords, and Generals, tho' they were Bas—ds at first" (5). Monmouth, Charles II's illegitimate son, was a focus for the hopes of anti-Jacobites, Defoe included, and his father was rumoured not to be Charles after all, but Colonel Robert Sidney.[19] It seems unlikely that the nurse could be alluding to the Duke of Berwick (1670-1734), the illegitimate son of James II who was brought up as a Catholic in France, since this would involve her in a glaring anachronism. But Defoe may have meant to remind his readers in 1722 of Berwick's Jacobite credentials: he fought for his father in Ireland from 1689 to 1691 and, through great generalship of the French and Spanish troops at Almansa in 1707, established the throne of Philip of Spain.[20] It is more certain that Defoe meant to draw attention, as he had done more than twenty years earlier in *The True-Born Englishman*, to the "lascivious" reign of Charles II, and the dukedoms conferred on six of his bastard sons at the country's expense.[21]

Jack is also made aware of the conflicts which continued to reverberate in England after the Restoration by his habit of listening to the reminiscences of old soldiers and sailors. Jack thrills to their romantic stories, and by the time he is fourteen he has learnt the names of all the ships in the navy, then, of course, under the future James II's command.

That Defoe wishes to associate Jack not only with the extremist Jacobites but with the high Tories generally is indicated by the sumptuous costume in which he dresses when he wants to deceive a Quaker clerk who has kept some money for him. Jack invents a name for his supposed employer, "Sir *Jonathan Loxham*" of "*Somersetshire*" (76) and, like his showy pink and green livery, this allusion suggests his attraction to the country party of knights and squires. The password of the gang to which he belongs, "GOOD TOWER STANDARD," evokes an image of defiance against the state, and it seems appropriate that when the foster-brother Captain Jack is beaten for his part in the kidnapping trade his punishment is administered by Sir William Turner, a prominent Protestant who lost his office under James II.[22] Captain Jack is as much associated with Jacobitism as the Colonel, for when he comes back from Ireland in what must be 1693 we learn that he was there for eighteen months; his stay must, therefore, have coincided with William III's campaigns against James II, culminating in the Battle of the Boyne. On returning to Scotland he joins the northern regiment led by Douglas, Earl of Arran, who was closely associated with the Jacobites.[23]

All this is, of course, to attribute a great deal of importance to passing references in the text, but we have already seen the extent of the ideological freight carried by casual allusions to recent history in *Memoirs of a Cavalier*, and it cannot be chance that Jack's life reminds us so frequently of the Jacobite threat: Defoe's references to real persons and events are never innocent. For example, when Jack and his boyhood friend Will steal a pocket-book, they discover that it contains bills from the following goldsmiths: Sir Henry Furness, Sir Charles Duncomb[e], J. Tassell and Sir Francis Child. As Samuel Holt Monk notes (313), all these men (except Tassell, who has not been traced) were in business when Defoe himself was young, but Monk omits to say that at least three of them are mentioned elsewhere in Defoe's writings, two with marked disapprobation. Sir Charles Duncombe was the alderman satirized in *The True-Born Englishman*, and Sir Francis Child was named in a letter to Harley in 1705 in which Defoe complained of the corrupt electoral practices of Child's brother, Josiah.[24] Geoffrey Holmes informs us that Sir Francis Child also made big capital gains by speculative dealings,[25] and Josiah is mentioned a number of times in *The Complete English Tradesman* (1726) as an example of rapid social ascent by a first-generation London financier.[26] Sir Henry Furness, ex-retail hosier, also features in *The Complete English Tradesman* (in the same breath as Duncombe),[27] and was unlikely to have appealed to Defoe since he had

103

endeavoured to support the Godolphin-Junto coalition in the summer of 1710 before Godolphin was defeated by Defoe's patron, Harley.[28]

The significance of these allusions is left for the reader to infer, but the indications of Jack's Jacobitism are often more heavy-handed. When threatened by imprisonment in Havana, Jack swears loyalty to "his *Catholick* Majesty," King Philip of Spain (279), and when he marries his fourth wife, Moggy, he calls on the services of a "*Romish* Priest" to perform the wedding service in what amounts to a priest hole (249). (Later this priest encourages Jack to join the Jacobites at Preston.) At one point, fearing Spanish privateers on the voyage from Virginia to London, Jack adopts Spanish colours for his merchant vessel and gives it the highly Catholic-sounding name of "*Nuestra Segniora de la Val de Grace*" (284).

Defoe's anti-Jacobitism is also at the bottom of his hero's conspicuous preference for words over fighting, for Defoe, both in this work and in others, capitalizes on the failures of James Stewart to carry through his planned campaigns. In *A True Account of the Proceedings at Perth* (1716), for example, the Old Pretender disgusts his followers by not engaging his enemies, and Colonel Jack himself is withering about both the Chevalier's "fruitless Expedition" (223) to Scotland in 1708, which ends in chaos, and the incompetent tactics of the Preston rebels in 1715, which have equally disastrous consequences for the Jacobite cause (265-66). Jack's indisposition for combat is symbolic of the fundamental pusillanimity which Defoe associated with the Jacobites.

Aside from the implicit ironies I have discussed, and ignoring the external evidence from Defoe's letters or from his other works, how were readers to recognize that *Colonel Jack* means to expose the fraudulence of its hero's claims to honour, and hence of Jacobites generally? Jack's gestures towards the Jacobites and the Catholic church are patently self-interested and insincere, as I have suggested, but in addition the "editor" makes plain in his Preface that Defoe's own religious and political values are Protestant, Dissenting and anti-Stuart.

Thus the Preface expresses a concern for the future of (nonconformist) charity schools, and places a Puritan emphasis on Jack's story as a "Parable" (2).[29] It is offered as "*a delightful Field for the Reader to wander in; a Garden where he may gather Wholesome and medicinal Plants*" (2). In the main narrative, too, there are several hints that Dissenting Protestantism is the source of moral and spiritual truth. As a child Jack receives sympathy and practical help from a clerk whose speech (e.g. 33) reveals him to be a Quaker; and in adulthood a reformed highwayman encourages him to try the Puritan practice of bibliomancy (divination by verses

104

of the bible) (169) and to read the Scriptures for himself (171). When Jack reviews his wicked life at the very end of the novel he acknowledges that his only sources of spiritual guidance have been this "Tutor" and also some "sober religious Company" (308) he encountered in Scotland, presumably Presbyterians like those Defoe befriended in his visits to Scotland in the 1700s.[30] Jack hopes his life story will be conducive to his reader's "moral and religious Improvement," recalling more orthodox and exemplary Puritan autobiographies, and declares that at last he has learned, "as *Job* says, *to abhor my self in Dust and Ashes.*"

At the heart of Defoe's hatred of Jacobitism was his Dissenting faith and consequent suspicion of any form of absolutism. His Puritan sympathies are evinced in his description of Jack's Virginian master, who combines the role of benevolent, contractual governor of his plantation with that of moral and spiritual mentor. He reminds Jack of the authority figures who overshadowed his youth in London: "he sat in a Seat like a Lord Judge upon the Bench, or a Petty King upon his Throne" (122). As such, he represents an ideal, being neither despotic nor brutal but paternalistic in his concern for his servants' moral welfare:

> I thought all my Master said was spoken to me, and sometimes it came into my Head, that sure my Master was some extraordinary Man, and that he knew all things that ever I had done in my Life. (121).

Jack and the other workers instinctively address this man as "your Honour" or "your Worship" (124), and he performs the offices of judge on several occasions, thereby illustrating the methods Defoe himself favoured in dealing with criminals: reason and moderation. But there is also some pointed dicussion of his political authority ("I abhor to be fear'd like a Lion, like a Tyrant, it is a Violence upon Nature every way" [144]), which suggests a desire to contrast him with the tyranny Defoe identified with Charles II and James II. When we recall the opening of Locke's *First Treatise of Government* (1690), Defoe's choice of a slave plantation for the setting of the Virginia section of *Colonel Jack* is thrown into relief:

> SLAVERY is so vile and miserable an estate of man, and so directly opposite to the generous temper and courage of our nation, that it is hardly to be conceived that an "Englishman," much less a "gentleman," should plead for it.[31]

Thus the humane and generous principles on which Jack's master, and then Jack himself, try to run the plantation should probably not be interpreted as signs of a disinterested proto-Abolitionism on Defoe's part, but as an indirect critique of the English monarchy before the Revolution of 1688-89. Although Jack tries to minimize corporal punishment of the Negroes, Defoe had too much interest in expanding England's colonies and trading interests in the New World[32] to offer any solution to the labour problem as radical as the outlawing of slavery. Jack himself ignores the ethics of the slave trade altogether, except for the question of whipping, and gives an unemotional account of the need to sustain a viable workforce:

> The Master whose Service I was now engaged in, was a Man of Substance and Figure in the Country, and had abundance of Servants, as well Negroes, as English; in all I think he had near 200, and among so many, as some grew every Year infirm and unable to Work, others went off upon their time being expir'd, and others died; and by these and other Accidents the Number would diminish, if they were not often Recruited and fill'd, and this obliged him to buy more every Year. (119)

Comparison with Howard Erskine-Hill's suggestion about the language of slavery used by Alexander Pope is helpful here, for he points out that references to New World slavery in texts such as *Windsor-Forest* were intended as coded allusions to Old World forms of government.[33]

In other ways, too, *Colonel Jack* is designed to show that the bitter political and sectarian divisions left by the Civil War have marked indelibly those who grew up during and after the Restoration. Jack was apparently born in 1682 or 1683, and by noting subsequent references to his age and the passing of time we can assume that his first violent crime was committed in 1690 and that he went to Virginia in around 1693. Defoe seems somewhat careless in having Jack remark that he lived in the colony for about twelve years (158), since this cannot be reconciled with the date given for his involvement in Austria's campaign against the French, 1701 (207), or with the fact that his "Tutor" worked as his manager for twenty years, up to 1716 (just after the Jacobite uprising). However, in broad terms the narrative connects Jack's childhood with the turbulent reign of James II; his youth with the period immediately following the Revolution Settlement; and his twenties, when he establishes his plantation and begins to export tobacco, with William III's campaigns against Louis XIV. He is back in England for both Jacobite uprisings, those of 1708 and 1715, but returns to Virginia when he realizes the dangers of associating with the rebels.

While I have already referred to contemporary fears of Jacobitism at the time of publication to explain *Colonel Jack*'s preoccupation with rebellion, it would be wrong to assume that Defoe makes no distinctions between the later seventeenth century and the 1720s. For instance, the narrative consciously evokes a London which is very different from that of 1722. Jack's descriptions of buildings and streets remind the reader that this is the city as it was in the wake of the Great Fire of 1666, when reconstruction projects included the Royal Exchange and the Custom House (both are featured in *Colonel Jack*) but when many archictectural landmarks familiar in 1722 had yet to appear. Jack and Will exploit the irregularity of the old City's street layout, and the proximity of fields which by 1722 had succumbed to property development:

> A Bag! *said I*, ay, ay, said he, let us get out into the Fields, where no Body can see us, and I'll shew it you; so away he had me through *Long-alley*, and Cross *Hog Lane*, and *Holloway lane*, into the middle of the great Field, which since that, has been call'd the *Farthing pye-house-field*: There we wou'd have sat down, but it was all full of Water; so we went on, cross'd the Road at *Aniseed Cleer*, and went into the Field where now the Great Hospital stands. (43)

In *A Tour Through the Whole Island of Great Britain* (1724-26) Defoe would celebrate the "New Buildings erected in and about the cities of London and Westminster and Borough of Southwark, since the Year 1666,"[34] devoting special attention to the achievements of Sir Christopher Wren, the sweeping away of the dangerously narrow streets of the old cities, and the building over of grass fields and "deep, dirty, and unfrequented" lanes (298). The *Tour* closely echoes *Colonel Jack*, though explicitly linking the fine new developments with the Glorious Revolution:

> To come to the north side of the town, and beginning at Shoreditch, west, and Hoxton-Square, and Charles's-Square adjoining, and the streets intended for a market-place, those were all open fields, from Aniseed-clear to Hoxton Town, till the year 1689, or thereabouts. (299)

In addition to its references to the urban landscape, *Colonel Jack* includes allusions to a number of historical personages who were prominent in financial and corporation circles in the Restoration period, from the judge Sir William Turner to a number of goldsmiths and aldermen already discussed. The old soldiers who entertain Jack with tales of long-ago campaigns remember "Oliver" and the execution of Charles I (11), perhaps indicating that they were members of the pro-parliamentarian London militia. There are other references to a specifically Restoration world: the kidnapping of innocent people (children in particular), for example, was an illegal trade peculiar to the period of Jack's childhood, presumably when insufficient numbers of criminals were being transported to supply the deficiencies of the Black slave trade. (This state of affairs would not have obtained when *Colonel Jack* was published some four years after the Transportation Act of 1718).[35] Defoe has Jack explain that kidnappers were

> a Sort of wicked Fellows that us'd to Spirit Peoples Children away, that is snatch them up in the Dark, and stopping their Mouths, carry them to such Houses where they had Rogues, ready to receive them, and so carry them on Board Ships bound to *Virginia*, and sell them. (11)

In minor ways, too, Defoe conveys a sense of London life in the 1680s; it is at Bartholomew Fair, which the Puritans had been unable to abolish, that Jack first learns pickpocketing, and with their ill-gotten gains he and his friend are able to make significant additions to their wardrobe. Wistfully remembering the old value of money, Jack notes that they bought two pairs of stockings for five pence, "and good Stockings they were too" (15).

These sorts of detail may be picturesque, but they serve a serious purpose in relating Jack's subversive activities as criminal and Jacobite rebel to the wider problems besetting society in the late seventeenth and early eighteenth centuries. Jack longs for an active role in public life, involving himself in a number of attempts to subvert the state, and his life reflects an aspect of early eighteenth-century politics which many writers from Swift and Pope to Defoe deplored: its polarization. Defoe wrote eloquently against putting party interests above those of country,[36] a vice to which he regarded Jacobites as especially prone.

Jack is worse even than many Jacobites, for his real concern is not so much party as himself. He is never completely open, even with those who are candid with him. He exploits his kidnapping, making much of the fact that he arrives in Virginia under very different circumstances from those of the average transport. Almost as soon as he leaves Virginia, the wider consequences of his self-absorption begin to manifest themselves. He has already shown a suspicious enthusiasm for the martial French king who has taken on the whole of Europe (172), and when his ship is captured by the French he shows his usual readiness to make the best of things, even if this involves collaborating with the enemy. When he reaches London he is greatly concerned to avoid recognition as a one-time criminal but sees no stigma in whole-heartedly embracing a French identity; in fact he declares he is "infinitely fond of having every Body take me for a *Frenchman*" (186). His first marriage having ended in divorce, he is soon eager to return to France, and once there he joins the side of Louis XIV, a decision which contrasts with his earlier reluctance to undertake military service. His descriptions of the European campaigns are an artful blend of self-promotion and pro-French propaganda, any victories by the "*Germans*" being regarded as the results of "Treachery" (207) or good luck (212). When the French army, despite outnumbering the Germans almost two to one, loses ground, Jack puts their failure down to German wiles (211). Though resolving that his own part in future campaigns should be minimal, he offers to raise supporters for the Jacobites in England and ends up joining the Chevalier de St. George in the expedition to Edinburgh in 1708. In this he is doubly fraudulent, for he is not even a convinced Jacobite, merely "pretend[ing] a great deal of Zeal" (222) for the Old Pretender, the Chevalier. When the expedition ends in chaos he is more grateful to escape arrest as a traitor than sorrowful at the failure of the rebellion, and can hardly wait to set foot again on French soil.

Once back in London he remains fascinated by contemporary politics; though the narrative does not mention specific dates, these were, of course, the turbulent last years of both Harley's ministry and the War of the Spanish Succession. Defoe clinches the case for interpreting Jack's private life as both shaping and shaped by his times through sly comparisons between his protagonist's experiences after his return to Europe and the great historical events which prompted his return. Under the protection of an English officer in Ghent, Jack had been lucky enough not to be captured as a prisoner of war, and armed with a French passport he was able to move with relative immunity through the battle-torn Spanish Netherlands. This habit of anonymity and detachment is continued when he resumes life as a private citizen in London, for he instinctively behaves as though behind enemy lines, and makes every effort to avoid recognition. Indeed, the account of his discreet enquiries about his old friends evokes the world of espionage, and sounds very like some of Defoe's letters to Harley during the Union campaign in Scotland:

> ALL these things I found Means to be fully inform'd of, and to have a long Account of the particulars of their Conduct, from some of their Comrades, who had the good Fortune to Escape, and who I got the Knowledge of, without letting them so much as guess at who I was, or upon what Account I enquir'd. (185)

It is ironic, given Jack's complete indifference to his public responsibilities as a citizen, that the language of the "public" spheres of war, diplomacy and espionage are a recurrent feature of his account of his time in London. Although he uses only his first name, and lives quietly, he comes to be well known and is eventually honoured with the military title (as yet quite unearned) of "Colonel" (185). When he becomes romantically involved for the first time, the application of "public" language to his private life becomes particularly striking, though he does not seem conscious of it:

> SHE attack'd me without ceasing, with the fineness of her Conduct, and with Arts which were impossible to be ineffectual; she was ever, as it were, in my View; often in my Company, and yet kept herself so on the Reserve, so surrounded continually with Obstructions that for several Months after she could perceive I sought an Opportunity to speak to her she rendered it impossible, nor could I ever break in upon her, she kept her Guard so well. (187)

Like Jack, his mistress conceives courtship as analogous to the conducting of international relations, believing that as the wife of a great merchant she will be a "Queen" (187), and maintaining that marriages should be

> only Treaties of Peace between two Neighbours, or Alliances Offensive or Defensive, which must necessarily have been carried on sometimes by Interviews, and personal Treaties; but oftner by Ambassadors, Agents, and Emissaries on both Sides. (188) [37]

Given the level of self-interest and deceit which accompanies their courtship, it is not surprising that Jack and his wife begin "a Friendly Treaty about Parting" (195) not long after their wedding. When Jack objects to her staying out all night, his wife angrily suggests that he gather information on her movements, and although he retorts that it is not his job to prove her honest, he does, in fact, set up a miniature network of agents (197) to provide "Intelligence" (198, 207) on her. The apt result of all this improper blurring of private and public is that Jack forfeits the protection due to the ordinary citizen and must finally, like a fallen leader, flee abroad to "be out of the way of Villains, and Assassinations" (204).

What Jack's marriage evokes in microcosm are the hostile relations between world powers who make treaties and alliances but who both cheat and distrust one another. Specifically, Jack's wife is reminiscent of Louis XIV, who broke the Treaty of Ryswick, which was negotiated by William III in 1697 and temporarily ended the War of the Grand Alliance. Jack's wife is suspect (in Defovean terms) in her attraction to things French, wooing Jack coquettishly and inviting him to practise the social skills of card-playing and dancing which he learned in France (191). Their marriage turns from a contracted peace into open war, and the "Treaty" (207) which Jack proposes for their reconciliation exposes him to further hostilities, perhaps reflecting Defoe's grave misgivings about the Treaty of Utrecht which ended the War of the Spanish Succession in 1713.[38] By insisting on Jack's marriage as a metaphor for, and also perhaps a product of, a war-riven era in European history, Defoe is making a moral and political point about the greed and dishonesty in human affairs at both levels, private and public. Through stratagems and shows of aggression, both nations and spouses try to advance their own interests, while in both cases total credulousness with regard to one's antagonist is an invitation to abuse.

In emphasising the significance of historical allusions in *Colonel Jack* we have seen that it is far more than an entertaining portrait of a plausible rogue; its aim is to demonstrate the connections between dishonest individuals and "Publick and National Mistakes and Errors in Conduct" (135). Jack is the inevitable product of a society divided by economic inequities and political factions. In adulthood he perpetuates the conditions which undermine his country's stability—and that of Europe—by conspiring directly and indirectly against his monarch. He has no conception of what is meant by duty, loyalty or self-sacrifice, and his career is one of endless deceit.

What Defoe offers with *Colonel Jack* is not just an historical novel, therefore, but a demonstration of how history is made. He rejects the tendency of individuals to deny their social and political instrumentality, viewing such denials as morally evasive. He depicts a world in which every action has its consequences, from the negligent administration of parish relief (a problem as urgent in 1722 as it had been in the 1680s) to the crimes of the most wretched pickpocket. As a child Jack is appalled by the devastation caused by his petty thefts—his victims lose irreplaceable documents along with their small change—and when he claims years later to have played key roles in European battles, or to have engineered the Preston rebellion practically singlehandedly, Defoe is not only showing how vain his hero is, but also stressing the genuine importance of the individual in determining the course of history.

The connection between the individual and the times in which he lives is made most suggestively when Jack describes his childhood fondness for listening to old men's stories, stories which boast of daring exploits in the service of the French king, and comments that "I was a kind of an Historian" (11). Making history and being made by it are impossible to distinguish here. Paradoxically, the personal ambition which makes Jack careless of his fellow human beings is what binds him to them and to his historical moment, for it proves that he is the offspring of that careless and divided society in the first place, even as he perpetuates its history of conflict and betrayal.

CHAPTER FIVE

Robinson Crusoe and the Value of Labour

So far it has been possible to show that a number of Defoe's narratives are dominated by similar ideological concerns (such as anti-Jacobitism, anti-absolutism and law-and-order issues), but the most famous of his works resists a similarly straightforward interpretation. Knowing about Defoe's political interests when he wrote *Robinson Crusoe* (1719)[1] cannot account for this, the best-known of his novels, for it is irreducible to anything remotely like a tract or a treatise (or even an economic plan). It has provoked diverse responses, being read by one critic as a study of "homo economicus,"[2] by another as a fictional spiritual autobiography,[3] and most recently as an allegorical rendering of England's liberation from the yoke of popery by William of Orange.[4] *Robinson Crusoe* is all of these and more, and while I cannot do justice fully here to the varied and complex meanings contained within it, I hope in these concluding pages to touch on some of the most important ones and to explain the relationships between them.

Unlike the novels which came after it—*Memoirs of a Cavalier* (1720), *Colonel Jack* (1722), *Moll Flanders* (1722)—*Robinson Crusoe* is not a sustained exercise in irony. While there is a modicum of irony in the fate which overtakes the hotheaded Crusoe once he has discarded his father's advice, and moments of irony in the story of his island incarceration—his illogical reaction to the discovery of some coins, for instance, or his terror at finding the famous footprint in the sand—Crusoe has more self-knowledge and self-discipline than the Cavalier, or Jack, or Moll, and on the whole the reader is encouraged to sympathize and identify with him.

At the same time, ideological, party-political, sectarian and economic interests have left unmistakable traces on this novel as on virtually all Defoe's narratives. *Robinson Crusoe* is opportunistic when, for example, it touches on the brutal conduct of the Spanish in South America, or makes a passing reference to the nature of tyranny, or raises the question of religious tolerance. All these are perennial topics in Defoe's work, and the manner in which they are treated in *Robinson Crusoe* is consistent with his treatment of them elsewhere. Moreover, the extent and geographical breadth of his protagonist's experiences enable him to address an unusual number of social and political issues, some more directly than others. For example, Paula Backscheider has traced the influence of the Salter's Hall controversy on the theological content of the novel, and she has also speculated about the relationship between Defoe and his eldest son as a template for the tension between Crusoe and his father.[5] In addition, the preoccupation with piracy which we find in *Captain Singleton* and *A Plan of the English Commerce* (1728) is evident throughout *Robinson Crusoe*, while the economic benefits of international trade are everywhere demonstrated by Crusoe's adventures, along with its pitfalls. To continue the list of issues raised in the novel, there is a reference to the Assiento (59), which reminds us of Defoe's lifelong concern with the failure of England to exploit fully the opportunities offered by the slave triangle, and some heavy-handed references to gambling (60), whose ethical and practical dangers had long worried Defoe.[6] Despite the worldliness of these subjects, *Robinson Crusoe* places an emphasis on the hero's introspection and piety, which some readers have found hard to reconcile with the hard-headed materialism elsewhere in the narrative. In a helpful monograph Pat Rogers summarizes the influence of travel literature on the novel, the importance of puritan autobiographies for Crusoe's spiritual regeneration, and the pervasive economic ideas which have led some critics to view the novel as an apologia for early capitalism.[7]

Not surprisingly, critics are at variance over the relative importance of these issues. My own view is that *Robinson Crusoe* was intended first and foremost as an indirect rejoinder to the proposals of the South Sea Company for dealing with the national debt in 1719, which is to complicate earlier readings rather than to offer an alternative to them. The following discussion begins by establishing the connections between the novel's various themes, and then shows how these relate to the issue of overseas investment. I will end, however, by emphasizing that *Robinson Crusoe* is much more than a vivid warning to financial speculators; indeed, it is uniquely successful among Defoe's works (with the arguable exception of *Moll Flanders*) in going beyond the immediate occasion of its composition.

Everything in *Robinson Crusoe*, the issue of speculation included, derives from Defoe's evangelical belief in travel as the ultimate source of adventure and, more importantly, wealth. Crusoe's father emigrated from Bremen to York, and Crusoe confesses to an almost compulsive urge to go abroad. As many commentators have noted, though he soon establishes himself in a profitable career as a plantation-owner, he is discontented by the remoteness of his situation and by the predictability with which his capital slowly accumulates. The punishment for his dissatisfaction will be banishment on a desert island, but even twenty-eight years in exile are not enough to stifle his "inclination to go abroad" (298), and the end of the first volume leaves him still aboard ship, shuttling between his Caribbean colony and Brazil.

Defoe's own addiction to travel is well documented. He had visited a number of European countries in his career as a merchant, and had toured extensively within Great Britain.[8] The mobility of his fictional protagonists is their most marked characteristic, and travel features in a number of his works published at around the same time as *Robinson Crusoe—An Historical Account of the Voyages and Adventures of Sir Walter Raleigh* (1720) and *Captain Singleton* (1720), to name but two. The travel tale was, of course, among the most popular literary forms of the eighteenth century, and scholars have shown that Defoe was acquainted with all the best-known examples of the sub-genre, e.g., William Dampier's *New Voyage Round the World* (1697), Robert Knox's *An Historical Relation of the Island Ceylon* (1681), and Woodes Rogers's *A Cruising Voyage Round the World* (1718). Some have argued that he also knew the Bermuda pamphlets on which Shakespeare drew for *The Tempest,*[9] and more recondite sources than these have been proposed for *Robinson Crusoe.* Almost certainly Defoe knew Montaigne, Hakluyt and Purchas.

Travel mattered to Defoe because it represented freedom and adventure, but most importantly because he regarded it as the key to untold profits. The natural and human resources of North and South America, Africa, and the Pacific Islands were endlessly advertised in his fiction and non-fiction, and the Spanish presence in South America was a constant source of irritation to him. One undoubted function of Crusoe's story was to promote travel and colonization, for Defoe regarded the English as deplorably lax in failing fully to exploit the opportunities for imperial expansion. When the hero leaves the mutineers on his island he is able to offer them a steady and abundant supply of corn, grapes, meat, milk and cheese; the only thing lacking, female company, he later remedies by sending seven Brazilian women to them. His island's bounty and fertility are continually emphasized; he finds "open or savannah fields sweet, adorned with flowers and grass, and full of very fine woods" (122), and reflects that he "had timber enough to have built a fleet of ships . . . grapes enough to have made wine, or to have cured into raisins, to have loaded that fleet when they had been built" (140).

Closely related to these advertisements on behalf of colonization is the theme of piracy. To Defoe, quite rightly, pirates were the scourge of British trade overseas, and from the *Review* in 1707, to *Captain Singleton* in 1720, to *A Plan of the English Commerce* in 1728, he sought to alert his readers to the scale of the problem and to propose various solutions to it. When a Turkish rover captures the ship which Crusoe sails as a "Guiney trader" and he is taken prisoner, the contrast between his life as a slave and the instant, huge profits he made from the gold he brought back to London is, in itself, a comment on the need for governments to stamp out piracy. When his island vigil is finally ended by the arrival of a Spanish ship, he is faced with quelling a mutiny in which an honest captain is about to be butchered. Both incidents emphasize that piracy is one of the chief hazards for the merchant (not to mention their hired skippers), making the business of transporting goods a high-risk one, and threatening the peace of Europe and its colonies.

Defoe is also anxious not to overlook piracy among English seamen themselves. His forbearance towards the Spanish in *Robinson Crusoe* is surprising—it contrasts strikingly with his hostile remarks about Spanish perfidy in *Captain Singleton*, for example—but it was almost certainly designed to draw attention to the barbarity of the English, who might otherwise have been tempted to consider themselves merely the victims of piracy rather than also, at times, its perpetrators. Crusoe reluctantly acknowledges that all the men in the long-boat which arrives on his island are English: "one or two I thought were Dutch, but it did not prove so" (249). Unlike Singleton, he is unequivocally on the side of the legitimate trader. Associating closely with a number of trustworthy captains in the course of his travels, he regards pirates as arbitrary and brutish, deserving of the harshest retribution.

Crusoe's remorseless treatment of the English mutineers, along with his vengeful impulses towards the cannibals, has been seen by some to conflict with his otherwise humane, Christian response to Friday, Friday's father, and the Spanish captain, raising the problem of how to reconcile the novel's emphasis on the importance of religious faith with its pragmatism and materialism. The apparent contradiction has been seen to be matched by equally glaring discrepancies between Crusoe's belief in divine providence, and his assiduous accumulation of material possessions on his island.[10] However, as I have argued elsewhere in this study, such contradictions are not exclusive to Defoe but deeply embedded in the Protestant ethic. The drive to work and to prosper is central to godliness, but spiritual faith too is a crucial reward for Crusoe and—

along with his huge stockpile—compensates significantly for his solitude. Equally, the impulse to exact revenge on Friday's tormentors is, paradoxically, a sign of his innate and commendable sense of justice.

Defoe's concern with the practical dangers and rewards of travel is, therefore, partnered by a concern for its ethical and spiritual implications. No less—and no more—important to Crusoe than his gunpowder or his barrel of biscuits is his Bible, the study of which, in conjunction with his situation, is enough to bring about his spiritual rebirth. Without a church (it does not occur to him to set aside part of his fortification for the purposes of worship), or even a biblical commentary, he effects his own conversion:

> This was the first time that I could say, in the true sense of the words, that I prayed in all my life; for now I prayed with a sense of my condition, and with a true scripture view of hope founded on the encouragement of the word of God; and from this time, I may say, I began to have hope that God would hear me. (111)

Backscheider (*Life* 417-20) contextualizes the story of Crusoe's spiritual self-education by highlighting the Salters' Hall controversy (1719) in which Defoe was involved. It centred on the question of whether Scripture alone was adequate to resolve points of doctrine; for Defoe and others the use of any other texts was tantamount to denying the truth of the Bible, and one step short of Rome in threatening to insert a priest or dogma between the believer and God. *Robinson Crusoe* itself serves as a repository of homespun philosophy and pious wisdom (which is how Wilkie Collins's Gabriel Betteredge read it),[11] and is self-evidently aimed at the lay reader. As Backscheider explains, it "illustrates deliberately and in great detail that Scripture and revelation without dogma are sufficient" (417). Indeed, one can imagine no more vivid image of faith through Scripture and revelation than Defoe's hero, deprived of any spiritual comforts save his New Testament and his sense of Providential deliverance. Nonetheless, Defoe was not simply reacting to a specific incident: the Salters' Hall controversy may have lent greater piquancy to Crusoe's intimations of faith, but the idea of the solitary penitent wrestling with his or her God is central to Reformation theology, and features in many of Defoe's novels, including one, *Roxana* (1724), written five years after *Robinson Crusoe*.

It seems likewise unnecessary to search, as some critics have done, for detailed parallels between Crusoe's experiences and those of England in the seventeenth century.[12] Though the twenty-eight years of the hero's

— so not the Dutch !

exile correspond exactly to the twenty-eight years of Stuart rule, and the rescue by the Spanish puts an end to the tyrannical behaviour of the English mutineers, such echoes are not sounded systematically, and are suggested rather than underlined. It is true, however, that, just as Protestant ideas of faith and Scriptural authority pervade the narrative, so too do anti-absolutist principles. In fact, Protestantism and democratic politics are implicitly linked when Crusoe reflects on the practices of the Caribs:

> I observed that there is priestcraft even amongst the most blinded ignorant pagans in the world; and the policy of making a secret religion, in order to preserve the veneration of the people to the clergy, is not only to be found in the Roman, but perhaps among all religions in the world, even among the most brutish and barbarous savages. (219)

Of course Crusoe proves susceptible to the temptations of absolutism himself, delighting firstly in his mock-monarchical rule over his land and pets, and then in his actual, if microcosmic rule over Friday, Friday's father, and the Spanish castaways. Although, as he proudly points out, he "allowed liberty of conscience throughout [his] dominions" (241; in contrast to the imposition of Catholicism by the Spanish on all their Brazilian subjects), his authority is total and his language self-consciously political. He is alert to the dangers of plots and conspiracies, savours the extent of his property rights, and regards himself as an instrument of God.

He is not, however, an absolutist in the Stuart sense, since his religious tolerance is unlimited, and the punishments he inflicts on wrongdoers, though severe, are the opposite of arbitrary. He is also politically astute, allowing the rebel Englishmen to believe that he is merely the agent of the island's governor, and remaining open to advice from those close to him. He is far too canny to take risks at the first chance of freedom, confiding his fears openly to the Spanish captain:

> I told him with freedom, I feared mostly their [i.e. the Spanish and Portuguese castaways'] treachery and ill usage of me, if I put my life in their hands, for that gratitude was no inherent virtue in the nature of man; nor did men always square their dealings by the obligations they had received, so much as they did by the advantages they expected. (243)

He is no tyrant, but no idealist either. As in _Captain Singleton_, a strong sense of natural justice is combined with a Hobbesian conviction in the baseness of human nature. After duly deliberating, Crusoe decides to flog, then pardon two of the mutineers who wish to return home with

118

their newly restored captain. Clearly he believes in both the efficacy of corporal punishment and the capacity of criminals to reform.

Even this very brief consideration of the various thematic strands of *Robinson Crusoe* reveals their inter-connectedness as well as the range of Defoe's interests in the novel. Travel raises issues of trade, colonization, piracy, religious belief, and political theory, most of which are mutually reinforcing: piracy, for example, suggests a parallel with political tyranny in legitimate commonwealths, while religious belief cannot be divorced from the question of the rights of the individual. In the rest of this chapter I hope to show that a knowledge of *Robinson Crusoe*'s immediate context, specifically Defoe's reaction to the South Sea flotation, helps us to understand the relationships between its many themes more fully. My aim will not be to refute traditional interpretations of Defoe's story, but to suggest how apparently divergent readings of it may be reconciled. In brief, the question of speculation was an economic, moral and religious one for Defoe, and recognising that a particular stock-market crisis lies behind his novel helps us to understand his concern with both the practical aspects of Crusoe's experiences, and their spiritual and ethical implications.

That *Robinson Crusoe*'s central concern is with the ethics of overseas trade and, indeed, trade as an ethical imperative, is signalled by the name Defoe bestows on his narrator. The generic names Defoe gives to his protagonists provide us with clues about his aims in a number of his novels. Moll Flanders and Colonel Jack are perhaps the first examples which spring to mind, but—like "Bob" Singleton—"Robinson" is presumably intended as a type-name for a sailor. There is at least one other seafaring Robinson mentioned in the novel (264), and one recalls the "Bobby Shaftoe" of the folk-song. At the same time, a number of scholars have pointed to Defoe's schoolfriend and prominent Dissenter, Timothy Cruso, as one precursor of Robinson Crusoe,[13] so that the conjunction of "Robinson" and "Cruso" can be taken to suggest that the character is both a typical sailor and a man of deep religious convictions ("Crusoe" also, of course, puns on "cruiser"). As one might expect from the name of its protagonist, *Robinson Crusoe* contains all the key elements of a voyage narrative: skirmishes with pirates, shipwrecks, paradisiacal New World habitats, cannibals, Spanish traders, and a desert island. Moreover, Crusoe's psychological profile is a plausible one for somebody addicted to travel and adventure. His father left his native country in search of better trading opportunities, and settled in York, a thriving inland port. Defoe would later describe York in *A Tour Through the Whole Island of Great Britain* (1724-26) in these terms:

> No city in England is better furnished with provisions of every kind, nor any so cheap, in proportion to the goodness of things; the river being so navigable, and so near the sea, the merchants here trade directly to what part of the world they will; for ships of any burthen come up within thirty mile of the city, and small craft from sixty to eighty ton, and under, come up to the very city.[14]

Given this biographical and geographical background and, even more significantly, the proximity of Hull, then a major international port, it is not surprising that Crusoe develops a thirst for the sea. With hindsight he is conscious that his choice of career was predictable:

> But being one day at Hull, where I went casually, and without any purpose of making an elopement that time; but I say, being there, and one of my companions being going by sea to London in his father's ship, and prompting me to go with them, with the common allurement of seafaring men, viz. that it should cost me nothing for my passage, I consulted neither father or mother any more. (31)

We are right to expect a blend of the exotic, the marvellous and the thrilling from the ensuing account of Crusoe's adventures, but this is not to ignore the political, economic and religious dimensions of the text. Defoe's comments on rhetoric and narrative technique in works such as *Religious Courtship* (1722) and *The Family Instructor* (1715) indicate that he attached great importance to entertainment as a means to (moral) instruction, and in *Robinson Crusoe* his romantic leanings go hand-in-hand with his didactic aims.

Hence, whereas his predecessors Woodes Rogers and William Dampier had merely sought to impress their readers with the rich natural resources waiting to be tapped in the New World, and had generally avoided discussion of the ethical and spiritual questions raised by travel and colonization, Defoe seeks both to promote the benefits of imperial expansion and to emphasize its costs.[15] Crusoe's island is lush and fertile, and provides him with ample food and shelter for survival, but its resemblance to Eden is deceptive. Whereas Andrew Marvell had fantasized about the double bliss of living "in Paradise alone,"[16] a hard primitivism underlies the account of Crusoe's struggles: his pastoral idyll can be enjoyed only through strenuous exertion. Like the fallen Adam and Eve of Genesis 3:19, Crusoe finds that, literally, "In the sweat of thy face shalt thou eat bread," and the fortune he amasses by the end of the first volume is derived entirely from his Brazilian plantation; the island has furnished him with no more than a goat's-skin cap, an umbrella and a parrot.

Marx was, therefore, wrong to regard the novel as an illustration of capital's ability to ignore the real costs of labour,[17] for Defoe never allows us to forget that without the supplies from the shipwreck Crusoe would not have been able to build, bear arms, or (initially at least) eat a balanced diet. The only money he takes away with him is a handful of coins which he salvaged from the wreck, and but for the charity of the Spanish captain he would be scarcely fit to re-enter civilization. He is well aware of this:

> He brought me also a box of sugar, a box of flower, a bag full of lemons, and two bottles of lime-juice, and abundance of other things. But besides these, and what was a thousand times more useful to me, he brought me six clean new shirts, six very good neckcloaths, two pair of gloves, one pair of shoes, a hat, and one pair of stockings, and a very good suit of cloathes of his own, which had been worn but very little: in a word he cloathed me from head to foot. (270)

Throughout his sojourn on the island he tries, not always successfully, to overcome the technological problems of producing commodities without proper tools or the right raw materials, and even when he manages to negotiate these practical obstacles the results are far from satisfactory and obtained at great cost.

There might appear to be a contradiction between the portrayal of Crusoe, who takes the best part of a year to produce his first loaf of bread, and Defoe's insistence elsewhere in his work on the profits to be made from colonization. Even in *Robinson Crusoe* itself he draws attention repeatedly to the rapid and reliable profits to be made from the plantations of Brazil. In *A New Voyage Round the World* (1724) and *A General History of Discoveries and Improvements in Useful Arts* (1725-26), as well as in *Moll Flanders* and *Colonel Jack*, he wrote enthusiastically of the money to be made in the New World by those prepared to settle and invest there. *A General History* opens with a glowing tribute to those whose vision enabled them to found empires:

> The most glorious Empires in the World had their beginnings in the little Adventures of single Men, or the small Undertakings of a few; so the most flourishing Arts, the most useful which the World now boasts of, had their Foundations in small Things, and from thence have encreased, and been brought to their present perfection by the application of private Men, whose

inspired Minds have guided them to propagate useful Knowledge, for the good of Mankind.[18]

Yet, although the *General History* is punctuated at frequent intervals by references to the unimaginable wealth of natural and man-made products to be found in Africa, the Americas and the Indies, Defoe's consistent emphasis is on the industry and determination required to exploit them. The natives of these continents are condemned for their idleness and neglect, which "have turn'd the most delicious Countries, formerly *flowing with Milk and Honey*, into a Desolate Howling Wilderness" (4). What is needed is an infusion of European skill and energy; Africa, for example, is running with wine, oil, corn and salt, almost all of which is going to waste. Defoe exhorts his readers to see

> how great an Improvement of Trade it might be to the World to have the Continent of Africa put into the possession of the diligent industrious Nations of Europe, who were able, and had a Genius apt to cultivate the Soil, and raise the Product to the same height, which it may be, and has been at. (112)

The burden of *Robinson Crusoe* is exactly the same: the climate of Juan Fernandez is temperate, its soil is fertile, its game superabundant; but until Crusoe arrives with gunpowder, metal tools and modern agricultural know-how it might as well not have existed. And once there, Crusoe faces an uphill struggle for long-term rewards and little immediate gain. In *Colonel Jack* Defoe encouraged his readers with the thought that a transported criminal would be able to establish an independent plantation after serving his or her indemnity for seven years, but he acknowledged that Jack had crucial help from his former master, who lent him tools, building materials, and manpower. Likewise, Crusoe reflects that his condition would have been very different "if the good providence of God had not wonderfully ordered the ship to be cast up nearer to the shore" (141).

The seeming contradiction between Defoe's view of the colony as a source of wealth and his emphasis on the hardships of the imperial enterprise is therefore less puzzling than it seems. For Defoe the riches available to British colonists were unquestionably immense, and the pre-eminence of the Spanish in South America was a constant reproach to British indolence and inefficiency. Yet episodes such as the Darien disaster of 1699, in which Scottish investors lost millions through speculating on the profits of a fragile, ill-conceived expedition to Panama,[19] had left him justifiably sceptical about the ease with which colonies could be made to produce quick profits. He withdrew his own investments in the South Sea stock in 1719, and would view the stock-market mania of 1719, in which thousands of ordinary people were tempted to buy shares in the South Sea Company, with intense disapproval,[20] being staunchly opposed on both ethical and financial grounds to any form of gambling.[21] Throughout the summer of 1720 he would attack the recklessness of, as Backscheider puts it, "a nation infected by avarice." Backscheider notes that the tone of his writings on the sale of the South Sea stock grew increasingly outraged until, by September, he was willing to use the strongest terms to describe the conduct of investors:

> "The Biting, the Sharping, and Circumventing one another, practis'd . . . is like a Contagion," he wrote; many transactions are "shameless Fraud" in which "the Seller is a Cheat, for he takes the Price, and delivers nothing; the Buyer is a Cheat . . . on purpose to cheat another; and as he buys Air, so he sells a Bubble." (449)

Like the non-fictional writings contemporary with it—*Manufacturer* (13 October 1719–17 February 1720), *Commentator* (1 January–16 September 1720), *The Anatomy of Exchange Alley* (1719) and various essays in *Mercurius Politicus* (which ran from May 1716 to October 1720)[22]— *Robinson Crusoe* can be seen as a direct response to the frenzy aroused by the South Sea proposals. It highlighted the unrealistic expectations of the naïve and greedy investors, confronting them with the hard realities of founding colonies in remote and virgin territories. All the problems which beset the unfortunate pioneers in Darien and which made the success of the South Sea Company so unlikely—isolation, disease, hostility from the native population, the pirates who infested the high seas—are dealt with by Defoe in lengthy detail.

The presence of the Spanish is a further difficulty, and one which Crusoe is unable to overcome by himself:

> I knew there was no going to the Brasils for me, much less going to settle there, unless I resolved to embrace the Roman Catholick religion without any reserve; unless on the other hand I resolved to be a sacrifice to my principles, be a martyr for religion, and die in the Inquisition; so I resolved to stay at home, and if I could find means for it, to dispose of my plantation. (296-97)

The brutality of the Spanish in South America, and the efficiency with which their empire had expanded by comparison with that of the British or indeed any other European nation, were sources of aggravation to Defoe throughout his life, and as Pat Rogers notes, most of his references to Spain in works other than *Robinson Crusoe* are extremely hostile

(*Crusoe* 21). Such hostility is at first sight difficult to reconcile with the warmth with which Crusoe regards his companion and ally, the Spanish captain. This may, however, be explained as a reflection of Defoe's belief that in some respects at least the British would do well to emulate the Spanish, especially on a practical level. The Captain gives Crusoe sound advice about the feasibility of establishing a colony on his side of the island:

> he saw evidently what stock of corn and rice I had laid up; which as it was more than sufficient for my self, so it was not sufficient, at least without good husbandry, for my family, now it was encreased to number four: but much less would it be sufficient, if his countrymen, who were, as he said, fourteen still alive, should come over. . . . [H]e thought it would be more advisable to . . . wait another harvest, that we might have a supply of corn for his country-men when they should come; for want might be a temptation to them to disagree, or not to think themselves delivered, otherwise than out of one difficulty into another. (245)

The Captain ends his homily with a biblical quotation designed to reinforce the point about providing adequately for those we deliver from hardship, and the moral and religious dimensions of the imperial enterprise are clearly crucial to Defoe here, notwithstanding his relative indifference to the humanitarian issues raised by slavery or the seizure of native lands. What does concern him is the greed with which some contemporaries viewed the colonies, and their failure to anticipate the hard work which would be needed in the first years of any colony's existence.

Critics have argued over the relative importance of Crusoe's spiritual regeneration and his accumulation of property. The debate presumes that the religious concerns of the novel are fundamentally incompatible with its materialism; Crusoe stands accused of failing to see that his pious ejaculations are at odds with his compulsive hoarding of supplies. As *Moll Flanders* illustrates, however, a concern for the safety of one's property and a strong moral sense are complementary aspects of Protestantism, and it is entirely fitting that Crusoe should pursue spiritual and earthly rewards with equal tenacity. He learns a standard Puritan lesson on his island: to trust in God whilst recognizing that the Lord helps those who help themselves. As Michael McKeon explains, "in the historically transitional territory of early modern Protestantism, spiritual and secular motives are not only 'compatible'; they are inseparable, if ultimately contradictory, parts of a complex intellectual and behaviour system."[23]

124

While religious, moral and economic interests are seamlessly united in *Robinson Crusoe*, the story also enables Defoe to raise related issues of political philosophy. The hostility it provoked from the high Anglican Charles Gildon testifies to its success in articulating the political and sectarian views of the Dissenting merchant classes.[24] Crusoe's treatment of the unruly mutineers illustrates society's need for firm but just government, while his decision to respect his subjects' liberty of conscience confirms that a belief in the rule of law need not lead to tyranny. Crusoe is the opposite of a Stuart king: though resolute, he resists the temptation of absolutism, being willing to take advice from trusted companions, and preferring clever stratagems to brute force.

The happy outcome of his mini-war with the mutineers may even be attributed to the Whiggish equation of prosperity with an aggressive foreign policy. In Crusoe's view his authority over the Europeans who join him is justified by their prior descent into lawlessness, while Friday is right to submit to him because Crusoe rescued him from death. He also taught Friday Christian principles, and made him renounce the savagery of his own people, notably their cannibalism. In Defoe's terms, Friday is not enslaved but liberated by Crusoe. Having destroyed the cruel tyrants who would have killed Friday, he proceeds to govern him with kindness, reason and justice.

Robinson Crusoe is underpinned by the same political philosophy as *Captain Singleton*, then, and it is a philosophy consistent firstly with Defoe's lifelong opposition to political or religious absolutism, and secondly with his progressive belief in the capacity of the individual for amelioration. While his characters have a Hobbesian potential for brutishness, he also affirms law and justice as the guarantors of peace and prosperity.

In some respects Crusoe's island is like Gonzalo's ideal commonwealth in *The Tempest*, complete in itself. In other ways it is quite the opposite of the society envisaged by Gonzalo, for it depends on the hard graft of its citizen(s), and the strong leadership of its governor. Yet Crusoe is no Prospero; he reflects endlessly on his own conduct, and encourages pluralism rather than conformity amongst his "subjects." And unlike Prospero, but like Defoe, Crusoe is capable of ironic self-insight, recognizing his pleasure in his own authority and resisting the impulse, except where it is strictly necessary, to respond to violence with violence. His confidence in his own judgment is tempered by his openness to advice, and in any case reminds us that while Defoe loathed the Stuart kings, he was no enemy to monarchy in principle—quite the reverse. *Robinson Crusoe* is not a detailed allegory of the events of 1688, but the shadow of "William the Deliverer," who saved England from popery and wooden shoes, is, for one reader at least,[25] behind Crusoe's account of his "deliverance" (265) from incarceration.

According to the persuasive thesis developed by Lennard J. Davis, the early novel grew out of a "news/novels discourse" in which prose narratives of many kinds dealt with contemporary social and political issues. Out-and-out fiction was a useful means of disguising subversive comment in an age of repression, and novelists such as Defoe developed a strategy of coded irony in order to evade punitive new libel laws.[26] All the works by Defoe which I have discussed in this book bear out Davis's argument, and decoding their ironies has been a major aim of my project. Yet Davis also confirms the belief of many earlier critics in a qualitative difference between prose fiction before the early eighteenth century and those texts we identify with the emergence of the "modern" novel. In previous chapters I have been anxious to question the view that Defoe was more "inventive" or "realistic" or "modern" than his predecessors, but *Robinson Crusoe* is undeniably ground-breaking in its fusion of so many concerns, economic, social and religious, and in the primary importance it places on the reader's imaginative experience. The activities of the South Sea Company may have been its catalyst, but contextualization scarcely accounts for its astonishing success with generations of readers.

For a host of reasons, *Robinson Crusoe* has traditionally been singled out as the most significant landmark in the history of the early English novel. As far as this study is concerned, it stands alone in Defoe's oeuvre because, to a greater extent than any of his other works, it transcends the particular ideological issues which inform it. It may be inconsistent to end a study of Defoe's ideological agenda as it influenced his fiction with a shamelessly humanist affirmation of his literary genius, but it is just the kind of self-undercutting irony which Defoe himself is likely to have appreciated.

CONCLUSION

In this study I have been concerned to elucidate Defoe's political purposes and the methods by which he pursues them in his novels. *Memoirs of a Cavalier* reflects Defoe's anti-Stuart convictions at every turn, and exemplifies a technique which is characteristic of many of his works: the relentless re-envisioning of recent history. *Memoirs of a Cavalier* also illustrates Defoe's understandable preference for dealing with contemporary issues through suggestive but relatively safe parallels with the past: the Cavaliers of the Civil Wars irresistibly bring to mind the infatuated Jacobites of the 1710s and 1720s.

Colonel Jack adopts a similarly oblique approach; most of the action is set in the Restoration and immediate post-Restoration but suggests numerous useful lessons for the present. In addition *Colonel Jack* confronts its readers with the obligation to acknowledge their responsibilities for the course of 'history, and can therefore be seen to be founded on a proto-materialist understanding of the mutual determination of the individual and society.

Captain Singleton explores this relationship in still more detail, though this time relying less on empirical observation than on Defoe's knowledge of political philosophy. Singleton's travels allow him to encounter a number of constitutional models, from an absolutist regime to a contractual monarchy, each of which has implications for Defoe's view of the Glorious Revolution and the relationship between Parliament and the Crown under Anne and George I. The Scottish section of *A Tour Through the Whole Island of Great Britain*, which I have discussed only fleetingly in the present volume, shows the extent to which Defoe's representations of the "facts" could be partisan even when he was apparently eschewing fiction. Here the involvement of historical material and contemporary observation (not to mention sheer invention) is so intimate that it has successfully concealed Defoe's political motives ever since, and even those modern commentators who have drawn attention to his plagiarisms have not attempted to speculate about their motives except to suggest that Defoe was a hack who would cannibalize any previous text that suited his needs.[1]

From the idea of Defoe as an indefatigable commercial writer we are not very far from the idea that he wrote to serve various masters and was

127

conveniently lacking in political convictions of his own. I hope that the present study, which has highlighted the consistency of Defoe's political beliefs and ideological biases in a number of otherwise very different texts, has shown that Defoe might have been rhetorically accomplished but that he was very far from being indifferent to political questions. Indeed, one might argue that the more elaborate his strategies, the more committed he is to various causes, not the reverse. And the idea that he worked for both Tories and Whigs ignores the reality of eighteenth-century politics: he may have changed political masters, but in an age when party identities were only just emerging this was not necessarily indicative of substantive shifts in his position on particular issues. In any case, the incompatibility of Defoe as chameleon and Defoe as homely story-teller, two enduring themes of twentieth-century literary criticism, alerts us to the need for a more coherent account of his work.

In the light of research in recent years by Maximillian Novak, Paula Backscheider and others, the idea of Defoe as a crude practitioner of the early novel no longer seems tenable. A text such as *Robinson Crusoe*, for instance, is not so much primitive as endlessly perplexing: is it realist or romantic? Pious or materialistic? Lockean or absolutist? The chameleon label, on the other hand, has a certain usefulness in that it implies a continuity of identity—an essential Defoe—which is, however, concealed behind a series of masks. Where the chameleon analogy is less helpful is in associating Defoe with the crafty political survivor, for his masks were not assumed for his own protection but to enhance the effectiveness of his arguments.

Certainly Defoe published anonymously and pseudonymously, though there was, of course, nothing unusual in that.[2] But to say that he did so out of deceitfulness or cowardice is to miss the point. Disguising his identity no doubt saved his skin on a number of occasions, but his main reason for doing so, at least in the texts I have discussed, was his recognition that one persona is needed, say, to give an insider view of Charles I's supporters, another to expose the multifarious criminal activities afflicting Restoration society, and yet another to illustrate the dangers of abandoning a constitutional monarchy.

In the letter to Harley quoted in my Introduction, Defoe congratulated himself on the tactic by which he was gaining allies and confidantes in the conflict over the Union:

I have spies in the Commission, in the parliament, and in the assembly, and Undr pretence of writeing my hystory I have Every Thing told me.[3]

128

We might well recoil at this, and feel a pang for those who fell for Defoe's plausible guise as a historian sympathetic to their views. Yet I think such a reaction would be mistaken. Defoe's *History of the Union of Great Britain* would indeed be published, though not until two years later, in 1709, when its defence of the Union was retroactive. In the *History* Defoe urges reconciliation, and insists on the benefits the Union will bring to all sides. In 1707 it was handy for him to talk up the importance of his *History* and downplay its underlying motive, which was the passage of the Union itself. But neither concern is remotely sinister, though admittedly for some Scots any support for the Union would have been unwelcome.

The point is this: Defoe portrays himself as a historian; in other words, as an impartial collector and observer of facts. In fact he has a great deal invested in promoting a particular version of events, as we saw especially clearly when we examined *Memoirs of a Cavalier*. Nonetheless, though some of his stratagems may have been disingenuous we would be wrong to conclude that Defoe is cynical; his ultimate aim is always to convince people of views which he thought were in their best interest. A contextual reading of his works suggests not so much that he was duplicitous or Machiavellian but that historiography—and narratives generally, whether fiction or fact—cannot be other than subjective, particularly if they are written in response to current political, economic and social debates.

I would argue that Defoe is in some ways an admirable figure, both in the strength of his belief that individuals should and indeed do play a significant role in public life, and in the creativity with which he enacted such a role himself. Critics write of his "chequered career," and it is a metaphor he might well have liked, since it ably conveys the mobility, unpredictability and resourcefulness we associate with him, not only in his private life but in his public role as agent and most importantly in his writings.

It remains for subsequent research to estimate Defoe's success as a political campaigner, and at present we lack both the empirical and conceptual tools for doing so satisfactorily. This question the present study has left unanswered, largely because I have been reluctant to speculate about Defoe's contemporary readers and their responses to him. What is more feasible to offer here is a brief comment on Defoe's significance for the history of the novel, given my repeated assertion that his books are more lucidly understood as political interventions than as experiments in narrative form impelled by purely aesthetic and formal considerations. What happens to the conventional role assigned to

Defoe in the history of the English novel as a consequence of this altered emphasis?

In a sense very little; my preoccupation with his artistry belongs to a recognisable critical tradition. Like many others, I have emphasized his narratological complexities and his exploitation of various realist devices. My main quarrel with the view of Defoe as an "early master" of the English novel (leaving aside a host of other objections, such as the gender bias it reveals, and its neglect of the influence of the French romance) is that it ascribes to him a zeal for fictional innovation for its own sake, whilst ignoring his manifestly greater zeal for political affairs. Defoe may have become a progenitor of the modern novel in the late 1710s, but he did not do so with that distinction in mind.

The pamphlet he issued in his own defence *An Appeal to Honour and Justice* (1715), gives us an insight into his character which has resonance for his writings:

> it was about the year 1694 when I was invited by some Merchants, with whom I had corresponded abroad, and some also at home, to settle at Cadiz in Spain, and that with Offers of very good Commissions; but Providence, which had other work for me to do, placed a secret Aversion in my Mind to quitting England upon any account, and made me refuse the best Offers of that kind, to be concern'd with some eminent Persons at home, in proposing Ways and Means to the Government for raising Money to supply the Occasions of the War then newly begun.[4]

It is a familiar note, confiding and self-important, and it indicates the naïevety of overlooking sheer ambition in any account of Defoe's involvement in politics. And we do not need an extended consideration of Defoe's manipulations of historical "facts" to tell us that personal testimonies are inherently unreliable. Yet there is some value in his recollection, for it conveys the same restless desire to be at the centre of things which characterizes much of his writing and made this writing so audacious in its re-workings of recent history. It is perhaps appropriate to conclude a study of the "political" Defoe with a judgment which sounds somehow more suitable for a politician than a novelist: he deserves our admiration for his conviction and tenacity, even if his sense of civic duty was derived in no small measure from his personal vanity. Moreover, he may have had more impact on literary history than on affairs political, economic or social, but without the urge to influence contemporary events his achievements as a novelist would have been far fewer.

NOTES

NOTES TO INTRODUCTION

1 George Harris Healey, ed. *The Letters of Daniel Defoe* (Oxford: Clarendon, 1955) 210-11.

2 See J. R. Moore, *A Checklist of the Writings of Daniel Defoe* (1960; Bloomington, Indiana: Indiana UP, 1962). The influence of Moore's conception of Defoe is evident in the titles of Laura Ann Curtis's *The Versatile Defoe: An Anthology of Uncollected Writings by Daniel Defoe* (London: George Prior, 1979) and *The Elusive Defoe* (Totowa, N.J.: Barnes & Noble, 1984). Defoe was first compared to Proteus by Charles Gildon in the Preface to *The Life and Strange Surprizing Adventures of Mr. D—DeF—of London, Hosier* (London, 1719), rpt. in Paul Dottin, *Robinson Crusoe Examin'd and Criticis'd* (London: Dent, 1923).

3 P. N. Furbank and W. R. Owens, *The Canonisation of Daniel Defoe* (New Haven: Yale UP, 1988).

4 Michael McKeon, *The Origins of the English Novel 1600-1740* (Baltimore: Johns Hopkins UP, 1987) 316.

5 Paula R. Backscheider, *Daniel Defoe: His Life* (Baltimore and London: Johns Hopkins UP, 1989) xi.

6 Peter Earle, *The World of Defoe* (London: Weidenfeld and Nicolson, 1977) 4.

7 Lennard J. Davis, *Factual Fictions: The Origins of the English Novel* (New York: Columbia UP, 1983) 154.

8 Manuel Schonhorn, *Defoe's Politics: Parliament, Power, Kingship, and Robinson Crusoe* (Cambridge: Cambridge UP, 1991).

9 Rodney M. Baine, "Roxana's Georgian setting," *Studies in English Literature* 15 (1974): 459-73.

10 Lincoln B. Faller, *Crime and Defoe: A New Kind of Writing* (Cambridge: Cambridge UP, 1993).

11 Although Faller, for example, argues against the overdetermining view of Defoe as a self-conscious early novelist, he ultimately says little about the ideological factors governing Defoe's experiments with form:

> Defoe was not reaching toward the writing of novels, probably not even toward the writing of literature. He was improvising, making complex gestures in a complex moment with little aim beyond that moment; it is the complexity of his gesturing, the quality of his improvisation, that marks him off from almost

all other writers of prose fiction in his time, and from all other writers about criminals. (245-46)

[12] Ian Watt, *The Rise of the Novel: Studies in Defoe, Richardson and Fielding* (1957; Harmondsworth: Penguin, 1985) 66-151.

[13] See David Ogg, *England in the Reigns of James II and William III* (Oxford: Oxford UP, 1955) 3.

[14] D.[aniel De] F.[oe], *An Essay upon Projects* (London, 1697).

[15] See, for example, Katharine M. Rogers, "Fact and Fiction in Aphra Behn's *Oroonoko*," *Studies in the Novel* 20 (1988): 1-15; Robert L. Chibka, "'Oh! Do not fear a woman's invention': Truth, Falsehood and Fiction in Aphra Behn's *Oroonoko*," *Texas Studies in Literature and Language* 30 (1988): 510-37.

[16] David Macaree, *Daniel Defoe and the Jacobite Movement*, Elizabethan and Renaissance Studies 42 (Salzburg: Institut für Anglistik und Amerikanistik, 1980).

[17] [Daniel Defoe], *The True-Born Englishman. A satyr* (London, 1701). References in the text are to the tenth edition, which was published "with an explanatory preface," also in 1701.

[18] *The Foreigners: a Poem.* Part I (London, 1700). John Tutchin was a whig pamphleteer best known for his attack on Judge Jeffries in *The Bloody Assizes* (1689), of which he was chief author. (See James Bent, *The Bloody Assizes*, ed. J. G. Muddiman, Notable British Trials Series [Edinburgh and London: W. Hodge & Co., 1929].) According to the *DNB*, "Tutchin was much given to exposing scandals and to boasting of his own virtue and public spirit, and it is clear, from his relations with Defoe, that he quarrelled with political allies as well as opponents" (4:10). In 1704 Tutchin would be tried and found guilty of libel, though he escaped punishment through a technicality and subsequently died a debtor in the Queen's Bench prison.

[19] These are listed in the *British Library Catalogue*, under "Defoe (Daniel): Minor Single Works."

[20] Christopher Hill, "History and Patriotism," *Patriotism: The Making and Unmaking of British National Identity*, 3 vols., ed. Raphael Samuel (London: Routledge, 1989) 1:4.

[21] Swift asserts that "Satire is a sort of glass, wherein beholders do generally discover everybody's face but their own." *The Battle of the Books* is reprinted in Angus Ross and David Woolley, eds., *Jonathan Swift* (Oxford: Oxford UP, 1984) 1-22.

[22] Elie Kedourie, *Nationalism* (1960; London: Hutchinson, 1985) 67-73.

[23] Typically for Defoe, these casually dropped names were not selected at random. Sir John Houblon (d.1712), first governor of the Bank of England, belonged to a French Huguenot family (his father was an elder of the French Protestant church of London) and so epitomised the mercantile Whig interest sympathetic to William III. He was knighted by William in 1689 and elected lord mayor in 1695. His career is the antithesis of Sir John Duncombe's (see below).

Thomas Papillon (1623-1702) was a more provocative choice. A merchant and politician, Papillon was closely associated with the 1647 riot over the ordinance depriving the city of London of its militia. Like Houblon he was a French Protestant, and was held in ill favour by the court of James II, probably as a consequence of his opposition to the excise duty exacted on brandy. He was a loyal supporter of the country party, the *DNB* noting that "His candidature for the shrievalty of London [1682] . . . thus became the occasion for a trial of strength between the court and the country parties" (15:191). In 1684 he lost a case brought against him for libel: he had accused the incumbent mayor, Sir William Pritchard, of making a false return to a mandamus (a judicial writ) to swear him in as sheriff. In 1689 Papillon returned from hiding on the Continent and published a pamphlet containing a transcript of his trial and an appended "Matter of Fact Relating to Election of Sheriffs." The pamphlet indicates that Papillon's trial was a farce. In his summing up the judge appealed to the full authority of the state to justify his opinion that Papillon "had much better keep in [his] Counting-House . . . and mind [his] *Merchandice.*" He told the jury,

> You are to consider you give damages to the Plaintiff, not as Sir *William Pritchard*, but as Lord Mayor: And your severity in this Case, will deter all People from entring into Clans and Cabals to make disturbances, and affront the Government.

The name of Papillon must have had particular resonance for Defoe, self-appointed advocate for William, since Papillon had clearly experienced the rough justice the Stuart royal courts handed out to their opponents; his case also highlighted the nepotism rife in the city of London. See Ogg, *England in the Reigns of James II and William III*, 341, 348; see also *An exact account of the trial between Sir William Pritchard, Kt. and alderman of the city of London, plaintiff, and Thomas Papillon, esq; defendant; in an action upon the case at the sessions of Nisi prius holden for the court of King's Bench at the Guildhall in the city of London, on Thursday the 6th of November, 1684* (London, 1689).

Sir John Lethieullier (d. 1718) appears to have been a less notable figure, but his background, too, was Protestant and European, his family originating from Brabant. He had become sheriff of London in 1674 and purchased the Aldersbrook estate in Essex (a reference to which is contained in *A Tour through the Whole Island of Great Britain*, ed. Pat Rogers, 177).

Not only were Houblon, Papillon and Lethieullier shining examples of honourable, industrious Protestantism; the two former were associated with William's naval triumphs in the 1690s. They are appropriate choices, then, for a poem which extolls William's integrity and celebrates the success of his Continental campaigns.

24 In its view of female sexuality as driven more by financial than physical needs *The True-Born Englishman* is proleptic of *Moll Flanders* (1722) and *Roxana* (1724).

25 For Defoe Britannia may have had specifically Protestant associations. Madge Dresser argues that Britannia fell out of favour as a national icon under the Stuarts, who preferred the more masculine figure of Pallas. Perhaps significantly, Britannia made a rare appearance in 1628 at a civic celebration, the Lord

Mayor's Pageant organized by Thomas Dekker (Dresser, "Britannia," in Samuel, *Patriotism*, 3:26-49). One might also cite *Britannia's Pastorals* (1613) by the staunchly Protestant poet Sir William Browne of Tavistock. Browne is wistful for the past glories of Elizabeth's reign (Book II, Song iii), and elsewhere published "An epistle occasioned by the most intolerable jangling of the Papists' bells on All Saints' Night." See Gordon Goodwin, ed. *The Poems of William Browne of Tavistock*, introduction by A. H. Bullen, 2 vols (London, 1894). Dresser also notes that in one engraving dated 1688 Britannia is in possession of her religion and liberty under William III, who is shown trampling on a Catholic mitre and other symbols of popery. I suspect that William Camden's *Britannia* (1586) may have drawn Defoe's attention to the nationalist potential of the female warrior figure; later he would "borrow" from *Britannia* for his *Tour Through the Whole Island of Great Britain* (1724-25). See Pat Rogers, "Defoe as Plagiarist: Camden's *Britannia* and *A Tour Thro' the Whole Island of Great Britain*," *Philological Quarterly* 55 (1973): 771-74. Of course, Britannia was by no means the exclusive property of the Protestants; Dresser also points to her associations with the Virgin Mary (28-29). In the same volume Samuel discusses the contradictory uses to which some national mythic figures have traditionally been put. Robin Hood, for example, has appealed both to conservatives and radicals (Introduction, xiii). The phrase "radical patriotism" is borrowed from Linda Colley's "Radical Patriotism in Eighteenth-century England," in Samuel, *Patriotism* 1:169-87.

[26] See Backscheider 89. Defoe reissued his *Enquiry into the Occasional Conformity of Dissenters* when Sir Thomas Abney, after assuming the office of lord mayor, went to his usual meeting-house after attending St. Paul's in the morning.

[27] See Gulielmus Hogaeus, *In Obitum Magnæ Britanniæ Regius Gulielmi Tertii* (London, 1702), cited in the entry for Duncombe in the *DNB*.

[28] See Ogg, *England in the Reigns of James II and William III*, 87-89.

[29] See the *DNB* 6:177 and Ogg, *England in the Reigns of James II and William III*, 89.

[30] *DNB* 14:1190.

[31] *DNB* 2:286.

[32] *DNB* 17:913-21.

[33] The knights of medieval romance had an aristocratic aura which very likely enhanced rather than lessened their broad appeal as late as the early nineteenth century, as witnessed in the scores of chapbook versions of the Seven Champions of Troy, the Charlemagne stories and the Arthurian legends. See Margaret Spufford, *Small Books and Pleasant Histories: Popular Fiction and its Readership in Seventeenth-Century England* (London: Methuen, 1981) and Victor Neuburg, *Popular Literature: A History and a Guide from the Beginning of Printing to the Year 1897* (Harmondsworth: Penguin, 1977).

[34] Daniel Defoe, *The History and Remarkable Life of the Truly Honourable Colonel Jack*, ed. Samuel Holt Monk, new introduction by David Roberts (Oxford: Oxford UP, 1989) 5. *Colonel Jack* was first published in 1722.

35 Louise de Querouaille, for example, "was widely regarded by Englishmen and the French ambassadors as a representative of France at the English court" (K. H. D. Haley, *Politics in the Reign of Charles II* [Oxford: Blackwell, 1985] 15-16). Charles's secret treaty with Louis XIV in 1669 had contained a clause in which he affirmed his intention to announce his conversion to Catholicism in return for £200,000 from France. Historians still disagree in their interpretations of this affair, especially the extent to which it reveals Charles's supposed French and Catholic sympathies. See Paul Seaward, *The Restoration 1660-1688* (London: Macmillan, 1991) Chs. 3 and 4. David Ogg suggests it was the Triple Alliance which Charles signed with Louis XIV in 1688 that began "that process whereby Protestant Englishmen were to be welded together in the fire of hatred against France and the Papists" (*England in the Reign of Charles II*, 2nd ed., 2 vols. [Oxford: Oxford UP, 1963] 1:334).

36 Donald Bruce offers a corrective to this view, arguing that

> Some patriotic historians have averred that the court of Charles II learned dissolute habits during the long exile in France, returning to vitiate a blameless England. In fact, French manners during the minority of Louis XIV were particularly decorous and formal. Encapsulated by the court of Louis XIV, the former Cavaliers there preserved, in all their solemnity and authenticity, the conventions of the circle of Charles I. Restoration England was just the bawdy old England of Jacobean times getting going again with an initial violence. . . . The comic dramatists of the Restoration merely resumed the manner and the idiom of Ben Jonson, Thomas Middleton and John Fletcher. (*Topics of Restoration Comedy* [London: Gollancz, 1974] 15)

37 The *DNB* lists four daughters on whom Charles II conferred titles: Charlotte, countess of Yarmouth (her mother was Elizabeth Killigrew, Lady Shannon); Anne, countess of Sussex and Charlotte, countess of Lichfield (by Barbara Palmer); and Mary Tudor, countess of Derwentwater (by Margaret Davis). Other daughters were less fortunate (see *DNB* 4:105).

38 *OED*; Eric Partridge, *The Routledge Dictionary of Historical Slang*, abridged by Jacqueline Simpson (London: Routledge, 1973).

39 All information on Charles's illegitimate offspring is taken from the *DNB*. Modern biographies of Charles such as John Miller's *Charles II* (London: Weidenfeld & Nicolson, 1991) and Ronald Hutton's *Charles II: King of England, Scotland and Ireland* (Oxford: Clarendon, 1988), as well as primary sources such as Pepys's diaries, confirm that the four women singled out by Defoe were the best-known of the king's mistresses.

40 Colley, "Radical Patriotism," in Samuel, *Patriotism* 1:171.

41 Christopher Hill, "The English Revolution and Patriotism," in Samuel, *Patriotism* 1:163.

42 Ogg, *England in the Reigns of James II and William III*, 348-49.

43 *Letters* 128.

1 *Memoirs of a Cavalier* was published anonymously in 1720 and was first attributed to Defoe in 1784 by the publisher Francis Noble. The edition cited here is James T. Boulton's, with a new introduction by John Mullan (Oxford: Oxford UP, 1991).

2 The *Memoirs of Edmund Ludlow* (c. 1617-1692), prominent republican and regicide, were published for the first time in 1698-99. The text used here is ed. C. H. Firth, 2 vols. (Oxford, 1894).

3 Bulstrode Whitelocke's *Memorials of the English Affairs* was first published in 1682. As with Ludlow's *Memoirs*, the standard edition (in four volumes) is nineteenth-century (Oxford, 1853).

4 Edmund Ludlow's brother, for example, fought in the Low Countries (see his *Memoirs*, 1:28), and so did many others, though no complete list exists.

5 Edward Hyde, 1st Earl of Clarendon, *The History of the Rebellion and Civil Wars in England, together with an Historical View of the Affairs of Ireland*, 7 vols. (Oxford, 1849) 4:276-77.

6 See Lawrence Stone, *The Family, Sex and Marriage 1500-1800* abr. ed. (New York: Harper and Row, 1979) 164-65. There are sly digs at patriarchal fathers and employers in another of Defoe's novels indebted to Locke, *Captain Singleton*, as I shall show in the next chapter.

7 Clarendon confirms Defoe's verisimilitude in his explanation for his protagonist's career. Of Sir Richard Greenville (i.e., Grenville), Clarendon writes, "He was of a very ancient and worthy family in Cornwall, which had, in several ages, produced men of great courage, and very signal in their fidelity to, and service of, the Crown; and was himself younger brother (though in his nature or humour not of kin to him) to the brave sir Bevil Greenville, who so courageously lost his life in the battle of Lansdown. Being a younger brother, and a very young man, he went into the Low Countries to learn the profession of a soldier; to which he had dedicated himself under the greatest general of that age, prince Maurice, and in the regiment of my Lord Vere, who was general of all the English" (3:431).

8 See E. P. Thompson, *Whigs and Hunters: The Origins of the Black Act* (1975; Harmondsworth: Penguin, 1985).

9 Joseph Addison's *Remarks on Several Parts of Italy* (London, 1705), for example, celebrated Italian antiquities, and was a popular guide in the early to mid-eighteenth century.

10 In 1560 the States-General had Charles IX declare duelling a capital crime, and an edict of 1566 reiterated the death penalty for duellists. But the law was regularly flouted and pardons easily issued; V. G. Kiernan notes that eight thousand duellists were reportedly killed during the short reign of Henri IV (1594-1610). Louis XIII's chief adviser, Richelieu, clamped down on duelling

from the beginning of his ministerial career, arousing a public outcry when he refused to repeal the death penalty pronounced on two defiant young noblemen who had fought a duel in full view of Richelieu's own window in the Place Royale in 1627. Nonetheless, royal pardons continued to be granted to duellists by Louis XIII, in the face of Richelieu's disapproval. Kiernan suggests that the French aristocracy were unwilling to relinquish a custom which emphasized "the line of demarcation between itself and the obnoxious upper-middle class," a theory which may explain the middle-class Defoe's dislike of duelling (*The Duel in European History: Honour and the Reign of Aristocracy* [Oxford: Oxford UP, 1988] 75-77).

11 Jean Le Clerc, *Vie d'Armand Jean, Cardinal Duc de Richelieu*, trans. Tom Brown (London, 1695).

12 See M.S. Anderson, *War and Society in Europe of the Old Regime 1618-1789* (London: Fontana, 1988), and Geoffrey Parker, *Europe in Crisis 1598-1648* (Glasgow: Fontana, 1979).

13 As Paula Backscheider argues in *Daniel Defoe: His Life* (Baltimore: Johns Hopkins UP, 1989), the contrast was especially vivid for Defoe: "In the *Review* and other places Defoe had often compared the two Swedish kings and regretted Charles's lack of devotion to the Protestant cause that Gustavus Adolphus had defended so valiantly" (444).

14 Michael Roberts, *Gustavus Adolphus and the Rise of Sweden* (London: English University Press, 1973) 112. A detailed discussion of Gustavus Adolphus's military innovations is given by Michael Roberts, *Gustavus Adolphus: A History of Sweden 1611-1632* (London: Longmans-Green, 1953) 198-271.

15 Backscheider points out that in 1716 Defoe revised his poem, *The True-Born Englishman* (first published in 1701), and used the same arguments to defend George I that he had originally devised for William III (*Life* 387).

16 As a Dissenter, Defoe was pre-disposed to view the Scottish Presbyterians sympathetically. Backscheider argues that Defoe's *The Consolidator* is an unusually pro-Scottish work for an English author to have published during the difficult years before the union of 1707 (146). *A Tour Through the Whole Island of Great Britain* roundly condemns the episcopalian attacks on the Cameronians, the Reformed Presbyterians who rebelled against the government and were defeated in 1679. See, for example, the admiring reference to the Cameronian preacher, John Hepburn and the defence of the assassination of Archbishop Sharp in 1679 (*A Tour Through the Whole Island of Great Britain*, ed. Pat Rogers [Harmondsworth: Penguin, 1971] 594; 642). There is no doubt that there is a sharp discrepancy between Defoe's known views of the Scots and those of the Cavalier.

17 Introduction, *The General Crisis of the Seventeenth Century*, eds. Geoffrey Parker and Lesley A. Smith (London: Routledge & Kegan Paul, 1978) 2.

18 Parliament had also charged Charles with following "evil Counsel" in a motion of 20 May 1642 (Ludlow 1:36).

[19] The Cavalier may be exaggerating a little here; there were noblemen on both sides in the Civil War. On the other hand, Defoe's characterization of the king's forces differs little from that of G. E. Aylmer, *Rebellion or Revolution? England 1640-1660* (Oxford: Oxford UP, 1986): "From the start, he seems to have been better supplied with cavalry than infantry or artillery, and may have had a surfeit of officers in relation to other ranks, although young men of middling and even gentry and noble families served as volunteers in cavalry units, on both sides, especially in the socially prestigious lifeguards of the rival commanders-in-chief" (47).

[20] The Cavalier's sense that the king began the war with many advantages may be compared with Goldsmith's view: "Few princes ever ascended a throne with more apparent advantages than Charles; and none ever encountered more real difficulties. Indeed, he undertook the reins of government with a fixed persuasion that his popularity was sufficient to carry every measure" (Oliver Goldsmith, *An Abridgment of Dr. Goldsmith's History of England* [1764; London, 1821] 140-41).

[21] This is the Rupert of Roundhead propaganda, brutalized by Continental warfare and indifferent to English property and life. Modern historians agree that Rupert was often careless and clumsy, both in battle and its aftermath. See, for example, Peter Young, *Naseby 1645: The Campaign and the Battle* (London: Century, 1985) 31.

[22] As Bulstrode Whitelocke put it in his *Memorials*:

In human probability the king's army was the more likely to have prevailed, their horse more and better than the parliament's, and their foot near as good, their advantages greater, and their courages higher, and their confidence too much.

God was pleased to raise the courage of the parliament's forces, and to give them the success; and indeed all success in war, as well as in other matters, is the free gift of the Lord of Hosts. (1:217)

[23] This fictional incident helps us to reconstruct in imagination the extreme vulnerablity of private property to theft during the war. Aylmer suggests that "One of the minor mysteries of the war is how the two sides got enough horses, both for their cavalry and for transport needs" (52). The usual answer, and that supplied by Defoe, is theft from farmers and traders.

[24] Quoted by Godfrey Davis, *The Early Stuarts 1603-1660*, 2nd ed. (1959; Oxford: Clarendon, 1985) 141.

[25] The most famous of these was *Eikon Basilike, the Pourtraicture of His Sacred Majestie in his Solitude and Sufferings* (London, 1649), which purported to be by Charles himself. It was hugely popular and highly influential in presenting Charles as a martyr.

[26] Quoted by Davis (*Early Stuarts* 56), from Mary Anne Everett Green's biography of Elizabeth of Bohemia, forming part of her *Lives of the Princesses of England* (1849-51; London, 1854).

¹ *The Life, Adventures, and Pyracies, of the famous Captain Singleton*, ed. Shiv K. Kumar, introduction by Penelope Wilson (Oxford: Oxford UP, 1990); the quotation in my chapter title is from p. 11.

² Gary J. Scrimgeour, "The Problem of Realism in Defoe's *Captain Singleton*," *Huntington Library Quarterly* 27 (1963-64): 21-37.

³ A. W. Secord, *Studies in the Narrative Method of Defoe* (1924; New York: Russell & Russell, 1963) 112-64.

⁴ J. R. Moore, *Daniel Defoe: Citizen of the Modern World* (1958; Chicago: U of Chicago P, 1966) 252 n. 9; 275-76; 289; 311.

⁵ Manuel Schonhorn has published a modern edition of *A General History of the Pyrates* (Columbia: U of South Carolina P, 1972), but the attribution to Defoe has been questioned by P. N. Furbank and W. R. Owens, *The Canonisation of Daniel Defoe* (New Haven: Yale UP, 1988) 100-103, among others.

⁶ Timothy C. Blackburn, "The Coherence of Defoe's *Captain Singleton*," *Huntington Library Quarterly* 41 (1978): 119-36. Blackburn's targets are Ian Watt in *The Rise of the Novel: Studies in Defoe, Richardson and Fielding* (Berkeley and Los Angeles: U of California P, 1957) and James Sutherland in *Daniel Defoe: A Critical Study* (Cambridge, Mass.: Harvard UP, 1971).

⁷ Maximillian E. Novak, "Defoe's Theory of Fiction," *Studies in Philology* 61 (1964): 650-68.

⁸ Daniel Defoe, *A Review of the State of the British Nation*, ed. Arthur W. Secord, vol. 4 (New York: Columbia UP, 1938) 475 (No. 107; 18 October 1707).

⁹ As Maximillian E. Novak points out in *Economics and the Fiction of Daniel Defoe* (Berkeley and Los Angeles: U of California P, 1962) 108-109.

¹⁰ J. Paul Hunter, *Before Novels: The Cultural Contexts of Eighteenth-Century Fiction* (New York: Norton, 1990) 196-97.

¹¹ Daniel Defoe, *A Journal of the Plague Year*, ed. Anthony Burgess and Christopher Bristow (Harmondsworth: Penguin, 1966) 96.

¹² Thomas N. Corns, *Uncloistered Virtue: English Political Literature 1640-1660* (Oxford: Clarendon, 1992) 4. Cf. Singleton's subsequent account of his acceptance of the offer to turn pirate: "He then asked me if I would swear to be secret and that if I did not agree to what he proposed, I would nevertheless never betray him; I readily bound my self to that, upon the most solemn Imprecations and Curses that the Devil and both of us could invent" (138).

¹³ Stephen N. Zwicker, *Lines of Authority: Politics and English Literary Culture 1649-1689* (Ithaca: Cornell UP, 1993), Ch. 5; Howard Erskine-Hill, "Pope and Slavery." Alexander Pope: World and Work. British Academy Conference. London, 27 May 1994.

¹⁴ John Locke, *Two Treatises on Government*, introduction by W. S. Carpenter (London: Everyman, 1924) 3.

15 Aphra Behn, *Oroonoko: or, The Royal Slave* (London, 1688).

16 See George Guffey, "Aphra Behn's *Oroonoko*: Occasion and Accomplishment." *Two English Novelists: Aphra Behn and Anthony Trollope: Papers Read at a Clark Library Seminar May 11, 1974* (Los Angeles: William Andrews Clark Memorial Library, University of California, 1975).

17 The conduct of officials was a source of grievance to many during James II's reign, which witnessed an intensification of bureaucracy in areas of national life such as the excise. See Geoffrey Holmes, *The Making of a Great Power: Late Stuart and Early Georgian Britain 1660-1722* (London: Longman, 1993) 171.

18 Manuel Schonhorn, *Defoe's Politics: Parliament, Power, Kingship, and Robinson Crusoe* (Cambridge: Cambridge UP, 1991).

19 I have decided to follow eighteenth-century practice in this chapter, and use "men" and "man" when discussing theories of government. It seems to me that when Locke and Hobbes refer to "men" they mean precisely that, and not "men (and women)."

20 Holmes, *Great Power* 139-40.

21 Holmes, *Great Power* 160; Paula Backsheider, *Daniel Defoe: His Life* (Baltimore: Johns Hopkins UP, 1989) 48-49.

22 Richard Ashcraft, *Revolutionary Politics and Locke's Two Treatises of Government* (Princeton: Princeton UP, 1986).

23 Helmut Heidenreich, *The Libraries of Daniel Defoe and Phillips Farewell* (Berlin: Hildebrand, 1970). The *Two Treatises* appears in the catalogue for the sale of these libraries, though it is not, unfortunately, possible to identity which books were Defoe's.

24 Daniel Defoe, *The History and Remarkable Life of the Truly Honourable Col. Jacque, commonly call'd Col. Jack*, ed. Samuel Holt Monk, introduction by David Roberts (Oxford: Oxford UP, 1989) 33-40.

25 Joel H. Baer draws attention to the preoccupation of seventeenth- and eighteenth-century commentators with the "potential evolution of pirate communities into legitimate states . . . [with] governments capable of dispensing justice and of securing the common safety" ("'The Complicated Plot of Piracy': Aspects of English Criminal Law and the Image of the Pirate in Defoe," *The Eighteenth Century: Theory and Interpretation* 23 [1982]: 3-26). As a pirate Singleton seems a less ethical leader than he was in Africa, but he maintains some loyalty to the principles of justice and democracy.

26 For a helpful bibliography see Kumar's edition of the novel (xxiv-vi).

27 Furbank and Owens 100-114.

28 Backscheider, *Life* 47-48.

29 The *Spectator*'s pen-portrait of the fictional merchant, Sir Andrew Freeport, is helpful in understanding Defoe. Sir Andrew is

A Person of indefatigable Industry, strong Reason and great Experience. His Notions of Trade are noble and generous, and (as every rich Man has usually some sly Way of Jesting, which would make no great Figure were he not a rich Man) he calls the Sea the British Common. He is acquainted with Commerce in all its Parts, and will tell you it is a stupid and barbarous Way to extend Dominion by Arms; for true Power is to be got by Arts and Industry. He will often argue, that if this Part of our Trade were well cultivated, we should gain from one Nation; and if another, from another. I have heard him prove, that Diligence makes more lasting Acquisitions than Valour, and that Sloth has ruined more Nations than the Sword. He abounds in several frugal Maxims, amon[g]st which the greatest Favourite is, "A Penny saved is a Penny got." (Joseph Addison and Richard Steele, *The Spectator*, 7th ed., 8 vols. [London, 1724] 1:14-15)

30 Backscheider, *Life* 51.

31 Hugh F. Rankin, *The Golden Age of Piracy* (Williamsburg, Virginia: Colonial Williamsburg, 1969) 146.

32 Basil Willey, *The Eighteenth Century Background* (1940; London, Peregrine, 1986) 17.

33 Elsewhere Defoe identifies Quakers with the ability to equivocate: in *Roxana*, for instance, the heroine dresses in grey and comments that "there was not a QUAKER in the Town look'd less like a Counterfeit than I did" (*Roxana: The Fortunate Mistress*, ed. David Blewett [Harmondsworth: Penguin, 1982] 256).

NOTES TO CHAPTER THREE

1 Most notably, Ian Watt, *The Rise of the Novel: Studies in Defoe, Richardson and Fielding* (1957; Harmondsworth: Penguin, 1985) 104-51; see also Watt's "The Recent Critical Fortunes of *Moll Flanders*," *Eighteenth-Century Studies* 1 (1967): 109-26.

2 See, for example, Maximillian E. Novak, "Conscious Irony in *Moll Flanders*: Facts and Problems," *College English* 26 (1964): 198-204, rpt. in *Twentieth-Century Interpretations of Moll Flanders: A Collection of Critical Essays*, ed. Robert C. Elliott (Englewood Cliffs, NJ: Prentice-Hall, 1970) 40-48; James Sutherland, *Defoe* (1937; London: Methuen, 1950) 239.

3 *The Fortunes and Misfortunes of the Famous Moll Flanders*, ed. Juliet Mitchell (Harmondsworth: Penguin, 1978) 216. Gary Hentzi, in "'An itch of gambling': The South Sea Bubble and the Novels of Daniel Defoe," *Eighteenth-Century Life* 17 (1993): 32-45, argues that Defoe detested gambling all his life.

4 The reader to whom this episode is directed is surely male. I have already written in this chapter of "we" the readers, but would not wish to ignore the differences between probable contemporary responses to the text. Defoe addresses a variety of readers in the course of the narrative.

5 Defoe, *The Family Instructor*, in *The Novels and Miscellaneous Works of Daniel Defoe*, 20 vols. (Oxford, 1841) 15:237.

6   Paula R. Backscheider, *Daniel Defoe: His Life* (Baltimore: Johns Hopkins UP, 1989) 364.

7   The *Review* had likewise emphasized the sins of the husband rather than those of the prostitute: "There is the debauched husband who, having a sober, young, pleasant and beautiful wife, slights and abandons her to take up with an ugly, a tawdry, nasty, and noisome strumpet, and convinces the world that lust is blinder than love. This sort of wretch has but one act of kindness to his wife which distinguishes him from other brutes of his kind, and that is coming home laden with vice and rottenness, he gives his honest wife an ill disease that lifts her out of the world, putting her out of his reach, and out of her torment altogether" (*A Review of the State of the British Nation*, ed. A. W. Secord, 22 vols. [New York: Columbia UP, 1938] 4:475 [No. 107, 18 October 1707]).

8   E. P. Thompson, *Whigs and Hunters: The Origin of the Black Act* (1975; Harmondsworth: Penguin, 1985) 196.

9   Defoe, *The Memoirs of Majr. Alexander Ramkins, A Highland-Officer* (London, 1719).

10 Defoe, *The History of the Remarkable Life of John Sheppard, Containing a particular Account of his many Robberies and Escapes* (London [1724]); Defoe, *The Life of Jonathan Wild* (London, 1725).

11 John Robert Moore, *A Checklist of the Writings of Daniel Defoe* (Bloomington, Indiana: Indiana UP, 1960) 201, 205, 219.

12 Because of the disparity between the novel's actual and purported setting, the map of "Moll Flanders' London" supplied in Edward H. Kelly's Norton Critical Edition of the novel (New York: Norton, 1973) is problematic.

13 Defoe, *Religious Courtship*, in *The Novels and Miscellaneous Works of Daniel Defoe* 14:180.

14 Douglas Hay, "Property, Authority and the Criminal Law," in Douglas Hay, et al., *Albion's Fatal Tree: Crime and Society in Eighteenth-Century England* (London: Allen Lane, 1975) 18.

15 Alan Macfarlane in collaboration with Sarah Harrison, *The Justice and the Mare's Ale: Law and Disorder in Seventeenth-Century England* (Oxford: Blackwell, 1981) 186-87.

16 Paula R. Backscheider, *Daniel Defoe: Ambition and Innovation* (Lexington, Kentucky: UP of Kentucky, 1986) 153.

17 Tobias Smollett, *The History of England . . . designed as a continuation to Hume*, 7 vols. (London [1794?]) 3:187.

18 John J. Richetti, *Popular Fiction Before Richardson: Narrative Patterns 1700-1739* (Oxford: Clarendon, 1969) 50.

19 *The Rise of the Novel* 35. By borrowing Watt's felicitous phrase I do not wish to imply in any way that he overlooked the context for eighteenth-century fictional realism; the opposite is self-evidently the case.

20 Michael McKeon, *The Origins of the English Novel 1600 to 1740* (Baltimore: Johns Hopkins UP, 1987) 21.

21 J. Paul Hunter, *Before Novels: The Cultural Contexts of Eighteenth-Century English Fiction* (New York: Norton, 1990) 185.

22 Lincoln B. Faller, *Crime and Defoe: A New Kind of Writing* (Cambridge: Cambridge UP, 1993) 148.

23 Which is not to say that either Defoe or the government were necessarily justified in regarding crime as an intractable problem. Recent historians have pointed out that eighteenth-century definitions of criminality were profoundly class-ridden.

24 *The Spectator*, 7th ed., 8 vols. (London, 1724) 1:2. This was published on 7 March 1711 [n.s.], so that Defoe's *Review* paper (No. VIII, No. 23) on the interpretation of dreams, published 17 May 1711, may have been a reply to it. The paper is reprinted in *The Best of Defoe's Review: An Anthology*, ed. William L. Payne (New York: Columbia UP, 1951) 195-98.

25 *Spectator* 3:106.

26 Defoe, *A Tour through the Whole Island of Great Britain*, ed. Pat Rogers (Harmondsworth: Penguin, 1971) 57-60.

27 The phrase "working girl" still has ambiguous connotations, as exemplified by the title of a recent Hollywood film.

28 Bram Dijkstra, *Defoe and Economics: The Fortunes of Roxana in the History of Interpretation* (London: Macmillan, 1987) 19.

29 John J. Richetti, "The Dialectic of Power" (28) in *Daniel Defoe's Moll Flanders*, ed. Harold Bloom (New York: Chelsea House, 1987) 19-36.

30 Defoe, *The Complete English Tradesman* (Gloucester: Alan Sutton, 1987) 86.

31 G. L. Apperson, *Bygone London Life* (London: Elliot Stock, 1903) 60-61.

32 Defoe would set out these rules more formally in *The Complete English Tradesman*.

33 Kelly 49 n. 4.

34 Maximillian E. Novak, *Defoe and the Nature of Man* (London: Oxford UP, 1963) 93, cited by Shirlene Mason, *Daniel Defoe and the Status of Women* (St. Alban's, Vermont: Eden Press Women's Publications, 1978) 38. Defoe's *Conjugal Lewdness; or, Matrimonial Whoredom* was first published in 1727.

35 In a section entitled "An Academy for Women" in *An Essay Upon Projects* (1696), Defoe had written a Protestant reply to Mary Astell's *Serious Proposal to the Ladies* (1694). Defoe supported better education for women, but did not want a rise in the number of convent schools.

36 "Defoe's Account" (247) in Henry Fielding, *Jonathan Wild*, ed. David Nokes (Harmondsworth: Penguin, 1982) 221-57.

37 Gerald Howson, "Who Was Moll Flanders?" *Times Literary Supplement* (18 January 1968): 63-64, rpt. in Kelly 312-19.

38 "Defoe's Account," in *Jonathan Wild*, ed. Nokes, 231.

39 As Howson points out (Kelly 318).

NOTES TO CHAPTER FOUR

1 [Daniel Defoe] *The History and Remarkable Life of the Truly Honourable Colonel Jacque, commonly call'd Colonel Jack*, . . . (London, 1722). All subsequent references are to the World's Classics *Colonel Jack*, ed. Samuel Holt Monk, new introduction by David Roberts (Oxford: Oxford UP, 1989). I have followed the practice of most critics in using the Anglicized version of the hero's name.

2 Paula Backscheider discusses *Colonel Jack* at length in both her critical study, *Daniel Defoe: Ambition and Innovation* (Lexington: UP of Kentucky, 1986), and her biography, *Daniel Defoe: His Life* (Baltimore: Johns Hopkins UP, 1989). It receives detailed consideration in Lincoln B. Faller's *Crime and Defoe: A New Kind of Writing* (Cambridge: Cambridge UP, 1993).

3 For Defoe on the subject of necessity see Maximilian Novak, *Defoe and the Nature of Man* (London: Oxford UP, 1963), Ch. 3.

4 An account of the charity schools controversy as it relates to *Colonel Jack* is given by David Blewett in *Defoe's Art of Fiction* (Toronto: U of Toronto P, 1979) 102-104.

5 See, for example, Donald J. Leinster-Mackay, *The Educational World of Daniel Defoe*, English Literary Studies, no. 23 (Victoria, B.C.: U of Victoria, 1981).

6 It is used as a primary source by, for example, David Ogg, *England in the Reigns of James II and William III* (Oxford: Oxford UP, 1955) 25.

7 The narrative offers only one firm date, which is 1701, the year of the French campaign in northern Italy in which Jack is involved after his time in Virginia (210-11).

8 For an account of the social and political circumstances surrounding the Black Act, see E. P. Thompson, *Whigs and Hunters: The Origins of the Black Act* (Harmondsworth: Penguin, 1975).

9 See Ogg, *England in the Reigns of James II and William III*, 392.

10 See, for example, Blewett; and David Macaree, *Daniel Defoe and the Jacobite Movement* (Salzburg: Institut für Anglistik und Amerikanistik, 1980).

11 Like Blewett (94) I disagree with Michael Shinagel's uncritical view of Jack's gentlemanly aspirations in *Defoe and Middle-Class Gentility* (Cambridge, MA: Harvard UP, 1968).

12 Michael M. Boardman, *Narrative Innovation and Incoherence: Ideology in Defoe, Goldsmith, Austen, Eliot, and Hemingway* (Durham: Duke UP, 1992), Ch. 2.

13 J. H. Plumb points out that "throughout his career as the King's chief minister Walpole had personally supervized the vast web of anti-Jacobite intelligence which he had created in Europe" (*Sir Robert Walpole: The King's Minister* [1960; Cambridge, MA: Riverside, 1961] 298).

144

14 Brian W. Hill, *Sir Robert Walpole: "Sole and Prime Minister"* (London: Hamish Hamilton, 1989) 119. Atterbury had led the High Church faction in Queen Anne's reign.

15 *The Letters of Daniel Defoe*, ed. George Harris Healey (Oxford: Clarendon, 1955) 454; quoted by Boardman 41.

16 The Test Act required all holders of crown, civil or military office to take communion in the Church of England and was therefore prejudicial to Dissenters, though some Dissenters were inclined to obey the letter rather than the spirit of the law.

17 See Maurice Ashley, *James II* (London: Hutchinson, 1977) for James's official appointment to the commission of Lord High Admiral in 1661 (74), his resignation following the Test Act in 1673 (98), and his effective resumption of the post in May 1684 (150).

18 Gilbert Burnet, *History of His Own Time*, abr. Thomas Stackhouse, introduction by David Allen (1906; London: Everyman, 1991) 190.

19 See George Roberts, *The Life, Progresses and Rebellion of James, Duke of Monmouth*, 2 vols. (London, 1844) 1:3.

20 See Charles Petrie, *The Marshall Duke of Berwick: The Picture of an Age* (London: Eyre and Spottiswoode, 1953).

21 The cynical observations of Jack's nurse may be compared with the approval of meritocratic social advancement expressed in *The Complete English Tradesman* (1726). Defoe does not object to sudden elevation if it is deserving:

> Thus in the late wars between England and France, how was our army full of excellent officers, who went from the shop, and from behind the counter, into the camp, and who distinguished themselves there by their merit and gallant behaviour. And several such came to command regiments, and even to be general officers, and to gain as much reputation in the service as any; as Colonel Pierce, Wood, Richards, and several others that might be named.
> (*The Complete English Tradesman* [1839; Gloucester: Alan Sutton, 1987] 217)

Despite Defoe's support for the Monmouth rebellion in 1685 he appears to have had little admiration for Monmouth as an individual, judging by a letter he wrote to William Penn in 1703:

> But This is Not Universally True for the People Sometimes Love by Antithesis, and Sho' a Generall Affection to One Person, to sho' Their Disesteem of his Enemy, and This May be Visible in the Case of the Duke of Munmouth, who Really had Not a Great Deal of Personall Merit. (*Letters* 41)

22 Turner is identified by Samuel Holt Monk in the notes to the Oxford edition (312).

23 See Ogg, *England in the Reigns of James II and William III*, 265.

24 Defoe, *Letters* 104.

25 Geoffrey Holmes, *British Politics in the Age of Anne* (London: Hambleton, 1987) 156.

145

[26] Defoe, *Complete English Tradesman* 210, 215, 216. Christopher Hill quotes John Evelyn's description of Child as "most sordidly avaricious" in *The Century of Revolution 1603-1714* (1961; New York: Norton, 1980) 184.

[27] Defoe, *Complete English Tradesman* 32.

[28] Holmes, *British Politics* 172.

[29] That allegory is a particular feature of Puritan discourse is argued by both Edwin B. Benjamin in "Symbolic Elements in *Robinson Crusoe*," *Philological Quarterly* 30 (1951): 206-11, and J. Paul Hunter in *The Reluctant Pilgrim: Defoe's Emblematic Method and Quest for Form in "Robinson Crusoe"* (Baltimore: Johns Hopkins UP, 1966).

[30] See Backscheider, *Life* 217.

[31] John Locke, *Two Treatises of Government*, introduction by W. S. Carpenter (London: Everyman, 1924) 3.

[32] Demonstrated, among other works, by *A General History of Discoveries and Improvements in Useful Arts* (1726-27), passim.

[33] Howard Erskine-Hill, "Pope and Slavery." Alexander Pope: World and Work. British Academy Conference. London, 27 May 1994.

[34] Abr. and ed. Pat Rogers (Harmondsworth: Penguin, 1971) 296.

[35] Backscheider discusses the history of transportation as it relates to Defoe (*Life* 485-89).

[36] In *An Appeal to Honour and Justice* (London [1715]), for example, he writes,

> It is many Years that I have profess'd my self an Enemy to all Precipitations in Publick Administrations; and often I have attempted to shew, that hot Councils have ever been distructive to those who have made use of them: Indeed they have not always been a Disadvantage to the Nation, as in King James II's Reign, where as I have often said in Print, his Precipitation was the safety of us all; and if he had proceeded temperately and politickly, we had been undone, *Felix quen faciunt.* (5)

[37] This, incidentally, echoes Defoe's prescriptive definition of a Secretary of State in a letter to Robert Harley [July-August 1704?] as one responsible "For Foreign Intelligence, Correspondence with the Courts Abroad, Mannageing, Settling, and Obtaining Confederates, Observing and Suiting affaires with the Circumstances and Intrest of Princes" (*Letters* 36).

[38] As he concedes in *An Appeal to Honour and Justice* (1715), passim.

NOTES TO CHAPTER FIVE

[1] Daniel Defoe, *The Life and Strange Surprizing Adventures of Robinson Crusoe* (London, 1719). All references in this chapter are to the the text edited by Angus Ross (Harmondsworth: Penguin, 1965).

2 Ian Watt, *The Rise of the Novel: Studies in Defoe, Richardson and Fielding* (1957; Harmondsworth: Penguin, 1985) 69.

3 G. A. Starr, *Defoe and Spiritual Autobiography* (Princeton: Princeton UP, 1965) 74-125.

4 Manuel Schonhorn, *Defoe's Politics: Parliament, Power, Kingship, and Robinson Crusoe* (Cambridge: Cambridge UP, 1991).

5 Paula Backscheider, *Daniel Defoe: His Life* (Baltimore: Johns Hopkins UP, 1989) 417-18, 423-24.

6 Gary Hentzi, "'An itch of gaming': The South Sea Bubble and the Novels of Defoe," *Eighteenth-Century Life* 17 (1993): 32-45.

7 *Robinson Crusoe* (London: George Allen & Unwin, 1979).

8 Rogers 25.

9 J. R. Moore, "*The Tempest* and *Robinson Crusoe*," *Review of English Studies* 21 (1945): 52-56, cited by Rogers 33.

10 Most famously by Watt, in *The Rise of the Novel*.

11 Wilkie Collins, *The Moonstone*, ed. J. I. M. Stewart (1868; Harmondsworth: Penguin, 1966) 39-41.

12 Schonhorn, *Defoe's Politics*, 148-49.

13 In particular, J. Paul Hunter, *The Reluctant Pilgrim: Defoe's Emblematic Method and Quest for Form in Robinson Crusoe* (Baltimore: Johns Hopkins UP, 1966) 47, quoted in the Norton Critical Edition of *Robinson Crusoe*, ed. Michael Shinagel (New York: Norton, 1994) 249.

14 Daniel Defoe, *A Tour Through the Whole Island of Great Britain*, abr. and ed. Pat Rogers (Harmondsworth: Penguin, 1971) 521.

15 Typical of Dampier is the description of a savannah in Juan Fernandez which could maintain "4 or 500 Families, by what may be produced off the Land only" (*A New Voyage Round the World*, quoted in the Norton *Robinson Crusoe* 229). Rogers draws the following unproblematic conclusion from the story of Alexander Selkirk: "And by this we may see, that solitude and retirement from the world, is not such an unsufferable state of life as most men imagine, especially when people are fairly call'd, or thrown into it unavoidably, as this man was, who in all probability must otherwise have perished in the seas" (*Life Aboard a British Privateer in the Time of Queen Anne*, ed. Robert C. Leslie [London, 1889] 59).

16 "The Garden," l. 64, *Andrew Marvell: The Complete Poems*, ed. Elizabeth Story Donno (Harmondsworth: Penguin, 1972) 101.

17 Karl Marx, *Capital*, trans. Ben Fowkes, introduction by Ernest Mandel (Harmondsworth: Penguin, 1976) 169.

18 Daniel Defoe, *A General History of Discoveries and Improvements in Useful Arts* (London, 1725-26), iii.

[19] For an account of this economic catastrophe see John Prebble, *The Darien Disaster: A Scots Colony in the New World 1698-1700* (New York: Holt, Rinehart and Winston, 1968).

[20] Backscheider, *Life* 449.

[21] Hentzi (39) attributes Defoe's "traditional" attitudes to frugality, self-reliance and gambling to his Dissenting heritage.

[22] All these are cited by Backscheider, *Life* 603, nn. 33, 34, 36.

[23] Michael McKeon, *Origins of the English Novel 1600-1740* (Baltimore: Johns Hopkins UP, 1987) 319.

[24] Charles Gildon, *The Life and Strange Surprizing Adventures of Mr D— De F—, of London, Hosier* (London, 1719). Rpt. in Paul Dottin, *Robinson Crusoe Examin'd and Criticis'd* (London: Dent, 1923).

[25] Schonhorn 140.

[26] *Factual Fictions: The Origins of the English Novel* (New York: Columbia UP, 1983), esp. 95.

NOTES TO CONCLUSION

[1] See, for example, Godfrey Davies, reviewing *A Tour Through the Whole Island of Great Britain*, ed. G. D. H. Cole, *Philological Quarterly* 8 (1929): 187-88; J. H. Andrews, "Defoe and the Sources of his 'Tour,'" *Geographical Journal* 126 (1960): 268-77; Pat Rogers, "Defoe as Plagiarist: Camden's *Britannia* and *A Tour thro' the Whole Island of Great Britain*," *Philological Quarterly* 55 (1973): 771-74.

[2] His best known pseudonym was Andrew Moreton. Paula Backscheider lists the works published under Moreton's name in *Daniel Defoe: His Life* (Baltimore: Johns Hopkins UP, 1989) 517.

[3] *The Letters of Daniel Defoe*, ed. George Harris Healey (Oxford: Clarendon, 1955) 211.

[4] *An Appeal to Honour and Justice, tho' it be of his worst enemies. By Daniel Defoe. Being a true account of his conduct in publick affairs* (London: [1715]) 5-6.

WORKS CITED

I. WORKS BY OR ATTRIBUTED TO DEFOE

Unless otherwise stated, the place of publication is London.

An Appeal to Honour and Justice, tho' it be of his worst enemies. By Daniel Defoe. Being a true account of his conduct in public affairs. 1715.

The Complete English Tradesman. 1726. Abr. ed. Gloucester: Alan Sutton, 1987.

An Essay Upon Projects. 1697.

The Family Instructor. 1715. *The Novels and Miscellaneous Works of Daniel Defoe.* Vols. 15 and 16. Oxford, 1840.

The Fortunes and Misfortunes of the Famous Moll Flanders. 1722. Ed. Edward H. Kelly. New York: Norton, 1973.

The Fortunes and Misfortunes of the Famous Moll Flanders. 1722. Ed. Juliet Mitchell. Harmondsworth: Penguin, 1978.

A General History of Discoveries and Improvements in Useful Arts. 1725-26.

A General History of the Pyrates. 1724. Ed. Manuel Schonhorn. Columbia: U of South Carolina P, 1972.

An Historical Account of the Voyages and Adventures of Sir Walter Raleigh. 1719.

The History and Remarkable Life of John Sheppard. 1724.

The History and Remarkable Life of the Truly Honourable Col. Jacque, commonly call'd Col. Jack. 1722. Ed. Samuel Holt Monk. New introduction by David Roberts. Oxford: Oxford UP, 1989.

A Journal of the Plague Year. 1722. Ed. Anthony Burgess and Christopher Bristow. Harmondsworth: Penguin, 1966.

The King of Pirates. 1719.

The Letters of Daniel Defoe. Ed. George Harris Healey. Oxford: Clarendon, 1955.

The Life, Adventures, and Pyracies, of the famous Captain Singleton. 1720. Ed. Shiv K. Kumar. Introduction by Penelope Wilson. Oxford: Oxford UP, 1990.

The Life and Strange Surprizing Adventures of Robinson Crusoe. 1719. Ed. Angus Ross. Harmondsworth: Penguin, 1965.

The Life and Strange Surprizing Adventures of Robinson Crusoe. 1719. Ed. Michael Shinagel. New York: Norton, 1994.

The Life of Jonathan Wild. 1725. In Henry Fielding, *Jonathan Wild.* Ed. David Nokes. Harmondsworth: Penguin, 1982.

Memoirs of a Cavalier. 1720. Ed. James T. Boulton. New introduction by John Mullan. Oxford: Oxford UP, 1991.

The Memoirs of Majr. Alexander Ramkins, A Highland-Officer. 1719.

The Novels and Miscellaneous Works of Daniel Defoe. 20 vols. Oxford, 1840.

A Plan of the English Commerce. 1728.

Religious Courtship. 1715. *The Novels and Miscellaneous Works of Daniel Defoe.* Vol. 14. Oxford, 1840.

A Review of the State of the British Nation. 1704-13. Ed. Arthur Wellesley Secord. 22 vols. New York: Columbia UP, 1938.

Roxana: The Fortunate Mistress. 1724. Ed. David Blewett. Harmondsworth: Penguin, 1982.

A Tour Through the Whole Island of Great Britain. 1724-26. Abr. and ed. Pat Rogers. Harmondsworth: Penguin, 1971.

The True-Born Englishman. A Satyr. 1701.

II. OTHER PRIMARY SOURCES

Unless otherwise stated, the place of publication is London.

Addison, Joseph. *Remarks on Several Parts of Italy.* 1705.

Addison, Joseph and Richard Steele. *The Spectator.* 1711-12. 7th ed. 8 vols. 1724.

Behn, Aphra. *Oroonoko; or, The Royal Slave.* 1688.

Browne, William. *The Poems of William Browne of Tavistock.* Ed. George Goodwin. Introduction by A. H. Bullen. 2 vols. 1844.

Burnet, Gilbert. *History of His Own Time.* 1715. Abr. Thomas Stackhouse. Introduction by David Allen. 1906. Everyman, 1991.

Clarendon, Edward Hyde, 1st Earl of. *The History of the Rebellion and Civil Wars in England, Together with an Historical View of the Affairs of Ireland.* 7 vols. Oxford, 1849.

Collins, Wilkie. *The Moonstone.* 1868. Ed. J. I. M. Stewart. Harmondsworth: Penguin, 1966.

Dampier, William. *New Voyage Round the World.* 1697.

Gildon, Charles. *The Life and Strange Surprizing Adventures of Mr. D— De F— of London, Hosier.* 1719. Rpt. in Paul Dottin, *Robinson Crusoe Examin'd and Criticis'd.* Dent, 1923.

Goldsmith, Oliver. *An Abridgment of Dr. Goldsmith's History of England.* 1764. 1821.

Locke, John. *Two Treatises of Government.* 1690. Introduction by W. S. Carpenter. Everyman, 1924.

Ludlow, Edmund. *Memoirs of Edmund Ludlow.* 1698-99. Ed. C. H. Firth. 2 vols. Oxford, 1894.

Marvell, Andrew. *The Complete Poems.* Ed. Elizabeth Story Donno. Harmondsworth: Penguin, 1972.

Marx, Karl. *Capital.* Trans. Ben Fowkes. Introduction by Eernest Mandel. Harmondsworth: Penguin, 1976.

Papillon, Thomas. *An Exact Account of the Trial between Sir William Pritchard . . . and Thomas Papillon.* 1689.

Rogers, Woodes. *Life Aboard a British Privateer in the Time of Queene Anne.* Ed. Robert C. Leslie. 1889.

Smollett, Tobias. *The History of England . . . Designed as a Continuation to Hume.* 1757-58. 7 vols. [1794?].

Swift, Jonathan. *Jonathan Swift.* Ed. Angus Ross and David Woolley. Oxford: Oxford UP, 1984.

Tutchin, John. *The Bloody Assizes.* 1689. Ed. Joseph George Muddiman. Notable British Trials Series. Edinburgh: W. Hodge & Co., 1929.

———. *The Foreigners: a Poem.* Part I. 1700.

Whitelocke, Bulstrode. *Memorials of the English Affairs.* 1682. 4 vols. Oxford, 1853.

III. SECONDARY SOURCES

Anderson, M. S. *War and Society in Europe of the Old Regime 1618-1789.* London: Fontana, 1988.

Andrews, J. H. "Defoe and the Sources of his 'Tour.'" *Geographical Journal* 126 (1960): 268-77.

Apperson, George Latimer. *Bygone London Life.* London: Elliot Stock, 1903.

Ashcraft, Richard. *Revolutionary Politics and Locke's "Two Treatises of Government."* Princeton: Princeton UP, 1986.

Ashley, Maurice. *James II.* London: Hutchinson, 1977.

Aylmer, G. E. *Rebellion or Revolution? England 1640-1660.* Oxford: Oxford UP, 1986.

Backscheider, Paula R. *Daniel Defoe: Ambition and Innovation.* Lexington: UP of Kentucky, 1986.

———. *Daniel Defoe: His Life.* Baltimore: Johns Hopkins UP, 1989.

Baer, Joel H. "'The Complicated Plot of Piracy': Aspects of English Criminal Law and the Image of the Pirate in Defoe." *The Eighteenth Century: Theory and Interpretation* 23 (1982): 3-26.

Baine, Rodney M. "*Roxana*'s Georgian Setting." *Studies in English Literature* 15 (1974): 459-73.

Benjamin, Edwin B. "Symbolic Elements in *Robinson Crusoe.*" *Philological Quarterly* 30 (1951): 206-11.

Blackburn, Timothy C. "The Coherence of Defoe's *Captain Singleton.*" *Huntington Library Quarterly* 41 (1978): 119-36.

Blewett, David. *Defoe's Art Of Fiction.* Toronto: U of Toronto P, 1979.

Boardman, Michael M. *Narrative Innovation and Incoherence: Ideology in Defoe, Goldsmith, Austen, Eliot, and Hemingway.* Durham: Duke UP, 1992.

Bruce, Donald. *Topics of Restoration Comedy.* London: Gollancz, 1974.

Chibka, Robert L. "'Oh! Do not fear a woman's invention': Truth, Falsehood and Fiction in Aphra Behn's *Oroonoko.*" *Texas Studies in Literature and Language* 30 (1988): 510-37.

Colley, Linda. "Radical Patriotism in Eighteenth-Century England." Samuel, *Patriotism* 1:169-87.

Corns, Thomas N. *Uncloistered Virtue: English Political Literature 1640-1660.* Oxford: Clarendon, 1992.

Curtis, Laura Ann. *The Elusive Defoe.* Totowa, NJ: Rowman and Littlefield, 1979.

———. Ed. *The Versatile Defoe: An Anthology of Uncollected Writings by Daniel Defoe.* Totowa, NJ: Rowman and Littlefield, 1979.

Davis, Godfrey. *The Early Stuarts 1603-1660.* 2nd ed. 1959. Oxford: Clarendon, 1985.

———. Review of *A Tour Through the Whole Island of Great Britain.* Ed. G. D. H. Cole. *Philological Quarterly* 8 (1929): 187-88.

Davis, Lennard J. *Factual Fictions: The Origins of the English Novel.* New York: Columbia UP, 1983.

Dijkstra, Bram. *Defoe and Economics: The Fortunes of Roxana in the History of Interpretation.* London: Macmillan, 1987.

Dottin, Paul. *Robinson Crusoe Examin'd and Criticis'd.* London: Dent, 1923.

Dresser, Madge. "Britannia." Samuel, *Patriotism* 3:26-49.

Earle, Peter. *The World of Defoe.* London: Weidenfeld and Nicolson, 1977.

Elliott, Robert C., ed. *Twentieth-Century Interpretations of Moll Flanders: A Collection of Critical Essays*. Englewood Cliffs, NJ: Prentice-Hall, 1970.

Erskine-Hill, Howard. "Pope and Slavery." Alexander Pope: World and Work. British Academy Conference. London, 27 May 1994.

Faller, Lincoln B. *Crime and Defoe: A New Kind of Writing*. Cambridge: Cambridge UP, 1993.

Furbank, P. N. and W. R. Owens. *The Canonisation of Daniel Defoe*. New Haven: Yale UP, 1988.

Guffey, George. "Aphra Behn's *Oroonoko*: Occasion and Accomplishment." *Two English Novelists: Aphra Behn and Anthony Trollope: Papers Read at a Clark Library Seminar, May 11, 1974*. Los Angeles: William Andrews Clark Memorial Library, University of California, 1975.

Haley, K. H. D. *Politics in the Reign of Charles II*. Oxford: Blackwell, 1985.

Hay, Douglas. "Property, Authority and the Criminal Law." *Albion's Fatal Tree*, by Douglas Hay, Peter Linebaugh, John G. Rule, E. P. Thompson and Cal Winslow. London: Allen Lane, 1975. 17-63.

Heidenreich, Helmut. *The Libraries of Daniel Defoe and Phillips Farewell*. Berlin: Hildebrand, 1970.

Hentzi, Gary. "'An Itch of Gaming': The South Sea Bubble and the Novels of Daniel Defoe." *Eighteenth-Century Life* 17 (1993): 32-45.

Hill, Brian W. *Sir Robert Walpole: "Sole and Prime Minister."* London: Hamish Hamilton, 1989.

Hill, Christopher. *The Century of Revolution 1603-1714*. 1961. New York: Norton, 1980.

———. "The English Revolution and Patriotism." Samuel, *Patriotism* 1:159-68.

———. "History and Patriotism." Samuel, *Patriotism* 1:3-8.

Holmes, Geoffrey. *British Politics in the Age of Anne*. London: Hambleton, 1987.

———. *The Making of a Great Power: Late Stuart and Early Georgian Britain 1660-1722*. London: Longman, 1993.

Howson, Gerald. "Who Was Moll Flanders?" *Times Literary Supplement* (18 January 1968): 63-64. Rpt. in *The Fortunes and Misfortunes of the Famous Moll Flanders*. Ed. Edward H. Kelly. New York: Norton, 1973. 312-19.

Hunter, J. Paul. *Before Novels: The Cultural Contexts of Eighteenth-Century English Fiction*. New York: Norton, 1990.

———. *The Reluctant Pilgrim: Defoe's Emblematic Method and Quest for Form in "Robinson Crusoe."* Baltimore: Johns Hopkins UP, 1966.

Hutton, Ronald. *Charles II: King of England, Scotland and Ireland.* Oxford: Clarendon, 1988.

Kedourie, Elie. *Nationalism.* 1960. London: Hutchinson, 1985.

Kiernan, V. G. *The Duel in European History: Honour and the Reign of Aristocracy.* Oxford: Oxford UP, 1988.

Leinster-Mackay, Donald J. *The Educational World of Daniel Defoe.* English Literary Studies, no. 23. Victoria, BC: U of Victoria, 1981.

Macaree, David. *Daniel Defoe and the Jacobite Movement.* Elizabethan and Renaissance Studies, no. 42. Salzburg: Institut für Anglistik und Amerikanistik, 1980.

Macfarlane, Alan in collaboration with Sarah Harrison. *The Justice and the Mare's Ale: Law and Disorder in Seventeenth-Century England.* Oxford: Basil Blackwell, 1981.

Mason, Shirlene. *Defoe and the Status of Women.* St. Albans, Vermont: Eden Press Women's Publications, 1978.

McKeon, Michael. *The Origins of the English Novel 1600-1740.* Baltimore: Johns Hopkins UP, 1987.

Miller, John. *Charles II.* London: Weidenfeld and Nicolson, 1991.

Moore, John Robert. *A Checklist of the Writings of Daniel Defoe.* 1960. Bloomington: Indiana UP, 1962.

———. *Daniel Defoe: Citizen of the Modern World.* 1958. Chicago: U of Chicago P, 1966.

Neuburg, Victor. *Popular Literature: A History and a Guide from the Beginning of Printing to the Year 1897.* Harmondsworth: Penguin, 1977.

Novak, Maximillian E. "Concious Irony in *Moll Flanders*: Facts and Problems." *College English* 26 (1964): 198-204. Rpt. in Elliott, *Twentieth-Century Interpretations of Moll Flanders.* 40-48.

———. *Defoe and the Nature of Man.* London: Oxford UP, 1963.

———. "Defoe's Theory of Fiction." *Studies in Philology* 61 (1964): 650-68.

———. *Economics and the Fiction of Daniel Defoe.* Berkeley: U of California P, 1962.

Ogg, David. *England in the Reign of Charles II.* 2nd ed. 2 vols. Oxford: Oxford UP, 1963.

———. *England in the Reigns of James II and William III.* Oxford: Oxford UP, 1955.

Parker, Geoffrey. *Europe in Crisis 1598-1648.* Glasgow: Fontana, 1979.

Parker, Geoffrey, and Lesley A. Smith. *The General Crisis of the Seventeenth Century.* London: Routledge and Kegan Paul, 1978.

Partridge, Eric. *The Routledge Dictionary of Historical Slang.* Ed. Jacqueline Simpson. London: Routledge and Kegan Paul, 1973.

Payne, William L., ed. *The Best of Defoe's Review: An Anthology.* New York: Columbia UP, 1957.

Petrie, Charles. *The Marshall Duke of Berwick: The Picture of an Age.* London: Eyre and Spottiswoode, 1953.

Plumb, John Harold. *Sir Robert Walpole: The King's Minister.* 1960. Cambridge, MA: Riverside, 1961.

Prebble, John. *The Darien Disaster: A Scots Colony in the New World 1698-1700.* New York: Holt, Rinehart and Winston, 1968.

Rankin, Hugh F. *The Golden Age of Piracy.* Williamsburg, VA: Colonial Williamsburg, 1969.

Richetti, John. "The Dialectic of Power." *Daniel Defoe's Moll Flanders.* Ed. Harold Bloom. New York: Chelsea House, 1987. 19-36.

———. *Popular Fiction Before Richardson: Narrative Patterns 1700-1739.* Oxford: Clarendon, 1969.

Roberts, George. *The Life, Progresses and Rebellion of James, Duke of Monmouth.* 2 vols. London, 1844.

Roberts, Michael. *Gustavus Adolphus: A History of Sweden 1611-1632.* Vol. 1. London: Longmans, Green, 1953.

———. *Gustavus Adolphus and the Rise of Sweden.* London: English Universities Presses, 1973.

Rogers, Katharine M. "Fact and Fiction in Aphra Behn's *Oroonoko.*" *Studies in the Novel* 20 (1988): 1-15.

Rogers, Pat. "Defoe as Plagiarist: Camden's *Britannia* and *A Tour Thro' the Whole Island of Great Britain.*" *Philological Quarterly* 55 (1973): 771-74.

———. *Robinson Crusoe.* London: George Allen & Unwin, 1979.

Samuel, Raphael, ed. *Patriotism: The Making and Unmaking of British National Identity.* 3 vols. London: Routledge, 1989.

Schonhorn, Manuel. *Defoe's Politics: Parliament, Power, Kingship and "Robinson Crusoe."* Cambridge: Cambridge UP, 1991.

Scrimgeour, Gary J. "The Problem of Realism in Defoe's *Captain Singleton.*" *Huntington Library Quarterly* 27 (1963-64): 21-37.

Seaward, Paul. *The Restoration 1660-1688.* London: Macmillan, 1991.

Secord, Arthur Wellesley. *Studies in the Narrative Method of Defoe.* 1924. New York: Russell & Russell, 1963.

Shinagel, Michael. *Daniel Defoe and Middle-Class Gentility.* Cambridge, MA: Harvard UP, 1968.

Spufford, Margaret. *Small Books and Pleasant Histories: Popular Fiction and its Readership in Seventeenth-Century England.* London: Methuen, 1981.

Starr, G. A. *Defoe and Spiritual Autobiography.* Princeton: Princeton UP, 1965.

Stone, Lawrence. *The Family, Sex and Marriage in England, 1500- 1800.* 1977. Abr. ed. New York: Harper and Row, 1979.

Sutherland, James. *Daniel Defoe: A Critical Study.* Cambridge, MA: Harvard UP, 1971.

———. *Defoe.* 1937. London: Methuen, 1950.

Thompson, E. P. *Whigs and Hunters: The Origins of the Black Act.* 1975. Harmondsworth: Penguin, 1985.

Watt, Ian. "The Recent Critical Fortunes of *Moll Flanders.*" *Eighteenth-Century Studies* 1 (1967): 111-17.

———. *The Rise of the Novel: Studies in Defoe, Richardson and Fielding.* 1957. Harmondsworth: Penguin, 1985.

Willey, Basil. *The Eighteenth-Century Background: Studies in the Idea of Nature in the Thought of the Period.* 1940. London: Peregrine, 1986.

Young, Peter. *Naseby 1645: The Campaign and the Battle.* London: Century, 1985.

Zwicker, Stephen N. *Lines of Authority: Politics and English Literary Culture 1649-1689.* Ithaca: Cornell UP, 1993.

ENGLISH LITERARY STUDIES MONOGRAPH SERIES

ENGLISH LITERARY STUDIES publishes peer-reviewed monographs (usual length, 45,000-60,000 words) on the literatures written in English. The Series is open to a wide range of scholarly and critical methodologies, and it considers for publication bibliographies, scholarly editions, and historical and critical studies of significant authors, texts, and issues. ELS publishes two to five monographs annually.